Genealogy of the descendants of Nicholas Hodsdon-Hodgdon of Hingham, Mass., and Kittery, Maine. 1635-1904

Andrew Jackson Hodgdon, Almira Larkin White

ANDREW JACKSON HODGDON

GENEALOGY

OF

THE DESCENDANTS

OF

Nicholas Hodsdon-Hodgdon

OF

HINGHAM, MASS., AND KITTERY, MAINE.

1635-1904.

PUBLISHED BY

ANDREW JACKSON HODGDON

EDITED BY

ALMIRA LARKIN WHITE

OF

HAVERHILL, MASSACHUSETTS.

HAVERHILL, MASS.

PRESS OF NICHOLS, "THE PRINTER"

—1904—

PREFACE.

This work has taken a considerable part of my time for nearly ten years, and has been quite expensive in many ways If a full year's time and the expenditure of two thousand dollars could have been given in addition for research in England, the complete English record of the family could have been secured, but I have not felt that I could afford either time or expense

I started with the idea, simply, of tracing my own line of ancestry, but have found this pleasant work leading me into so many other different lines that as a record of the Hodgdon family in America it is more complete than was at first intended

Thanks are due to Frederick M Hodgdon of Haverhill, Mass, also to Fordyce C B Hodgdon of Key West, Fla, who have kindly offered to share in the expense of publication, also to Miss Almira L White of Haverhill for the able and conscientious manner in which she has edited the book, and to all others who have kindly furnished information and pictures

In the years of expansion of this country the Hodgdon family has had its share, and in the pursuit of industry and commerce has gone into many of the states of the union Naturally the tracing of genealogical records has, therefore, met with some difficulties and the result is likely to fall short of being absolutely complete and perfect The following record is, however, the result of careful and persistent inquiry, and no line has been left until satisfactory information has been secured, or the futility of further inquiry demonstrated I trust that the book will meet with the approbation of the members of the Hodgdon family, that they may take pleasure in its reading, as I have in its preparation

ANDREW J HODGDON

Hodsdon of Hodsdon.

EXPLANATIONS.

In arranging this work it has been my object to give all the authentic history and genealogy of the first five generations of Nicholas Hodsdon and his descendants in the plainest manner The work is carried forward in the usual form to the fifth generation, then we have only attempted to trace the families of Maj Caleb and his brothers, Israel, Peter and John, and his sister, Abigail (Hodgdon) Peaslee

We find the name variously spelled and have copied it in every instance as we found it, one brother using the s and the other the g

The Arms of Hodsdon of Hodsdon, County Hertfordshire, England, were procured from Culleton's Heraldic Office, London They are inserted as the Arms of the family in England; although, for want of time and money, we have been unable to trace the English ancestry of Nicholas Hodsdon

ARMS Argent, a bend wavy gules, between two horse shoes azure

CREST A man's head couped at the shoulders proper, vested argent, on the head a cap or

MOTTO *Animo et fide* (By courage and faith)

I have made use of no unusual abbreviations, using those of months and states, also, b, born, bapt, baptized, m, married, d, died, p, page, vol, volume; dau, daughter Each member is numbered at birth, and when the name is followed by + it will be found again in its proper place with the birth number in a bracket at the right of the name If no + follows, all I could learn is recorded at the birth The small superior figure at the end of each name denotes the generation

EDITOR.

ILLUSTRATIONS.

ALMIRA L. WHITE

GENEALOGY

OF THE

HODSDON OR HODGDON FAMILY.

---

1. Nicholas Hodsdon of Hingham, Mass , 1635; and in 1636, the town of Hingham, granted him a house lot in the center of the town, and later, two or more meadows were granted him in the same town; reference is made to these meadows, in a deed given by Samuel Ward of Charlestown, Mass., to Edward Wilder, Mar. 30, 1665.

(Suffolk deeds, Vol. 4, p. 282.)

Nicholas was made freeman Mar. 9, 1636-7, (in the record the name is given as Hudson), he remained in Hingham until about 1650, when in company with John Winchester, Thomas Hammond, John Parker, Vincent Druce and others, he purchased large tracts of land at Cambridge Hill, now Newton, Mass., near the line which divides Brookline and Newton.

"Nicholas Hodsdin at Mr. Hibbins farme in Boston in Suffolk, hath souled to Thomas Hammond and Vincent Bruse (Druce) both of Hingham, in the same County, a parcell of land containing sixty seaven acres more or less, lying on Cambridge Hill adjoining to John Parker's to the North, Northwest and Northeast of the said John Parker's with thirteen acres more or less of meadow belonging thereunto, the which land was by the Towne of Cambridge given to Robert Bradish. Also sixteen acres in Boston bounds next to Cambridge Hill to the South of it, and to the East

and North east of Mr Hibbins' land, to have and to hold——— "
Dated, Feb 4, 1650, recorded, Aug 20, 1651
Middlesex County deeds, Vol I, p 24

"Nicholas Hodsdon of Boston to John Parker of Cambridge ——— a just third part of all the lands bought by him of Robert Bradish Wife Elizabeth gives her consent and yields up her right, Mar 20, 1651"
Dated, Aug 6, 16—, recorded, May 24, 1656
Middlesex County deeds

We find no deed or land grant between the above date and Oct 15, 1656, when he received a grant of land from the town of Kittery, Me, but seems to have been living there prior to that date as see grant below

"Granted, lotted and layed out by the Selectmen for Kittery unto Nicholas Hodsdon, his heirs and assigns forever, a lot of land above his house, bounded on the South side by Miles Thompson's land as may appear by several marked trees which go upon the line south east and by east unto the woods one hundred and sixty poles unto a tree marked four ways, and from said tree to go upon the line north and south and by east unto a marked tree Standing by the brook of Birchen Poynt and to come down the said brook unto the water or river, which brook is the bounds of said lot"
Dated Oct 15, 1656
Kittery town records, p 9

Dec 13, 1669, Nicholas received another grant of land from the town of Kittery, this lot being sixty poles in length, and adjoining Birchen Point Brook This lot was laid out Jan 1672

In 1673, Nicholas received still another grant of land from the town, which was for 100 acres of land This grant however was not laid out during his lifetime, but was sold by his descendants at various times

The following deposition of Nicholas and his wife is of interest, and shows that at the time they settled at Kittery, they resided at Quamphegon

"The deposition of Nicholasse Hodesden and his wife, aged 40

HOMESTEAD ON THE NICHOLAS HODSDON FARM

Said to have been built 200 years ago Now owned by Mrs. William Flynn

years and upwards. These deponents being sworne saith that fifteene or sixteene yeares agoe that Thomas Spenseer being at Quamphegon at the house wee lived in sayd. that he had given the one half part of the mill & timber thereunto belonging, being one quarter part of the mill unto Dariell Goodin for his dafters portion. Nicholas Hodsden & his wife replied & said, neybouer Spenser I wish you well to consider what you doe, for you had many children & every one would have a littell and you cannot give every one such a Portion, and he answered & said, that she was the eldest dafter & hee had don yt & farthersaith not." Dated, Apr. 18, 1670.

Nicholas purchased several lots of land in the vicinity of Birchen Point Brook. Peter Wittum sold him "forty acres of upland and swamp, butting upon the land of said Nicholas, and running back to Rocky Hills."

John Wincoll sold Nicholas "one Tenement with about 30 acres of land, bounded by land of Miles Thompson on the South, the River on the West and Birchen Brook and Cove on the North and highway that leadeth toward Sturgeon Creeke."

Dated June 16, 1674.

The farm which Nicholas occupied the latter part of his life, is undoubtedly the one just montioned as having been purchased of John Wincoll in 1674. It is situated upon the easterly side of the Piscataqua river, which divides Kittery from Dover. It is located in the extreme southerly part of South Berwick, and is bounded on the North by Birchen Point Brook ; on the south by the farm formerly owned by Miles Thompson. This last mentioned farm was bounded on the south by Thompson's Brook, which Brook divides the towns of Eliot and South Berwick.

The homestead, as will be noticed later, was given by Nicholas to his son Benoni, from whom it descended in regular gradation to John and Henry Hodsdon; who sold it to Theo. F. and Thomas Jewett, May 17, 1828, (York deeds, Vol. 130, p. 82.) at which time the estate passed out of the Hodsdon family. The Jewetts sold the entire farm to William Flynn by deed of Jan. 28, 1850,

(York deeds, Vol 210, p 449) and it is still occupied by the widow and children of Mr Flynn

"Agreement between Nicholas Hodsdon of Kittery, husbandman, and Benoni Hodsdon, son of said Nicholas, agrees that Benoni shall during the Natural life of Nicholas, have, hold and use in Partnership with his father, all that farm that his father has for several years lived upon, with all lands, medows, Orchards, Marshes, garden and all the privileges thereunto belonging or in any wise appertaining without any division of lands or houses, but in partnership and the same shall hold during the Natural life of said Nicholas

It is agreed that all of the stock of any nature heretofore belonging to the said Nicholas or Benoni are to be one half the said Nicholas and the other half the said Benoni

The said Benoni agrees to take the best of care of the farm and pay all charges and any profit arising from the product of the farm to be equally divided every year

It is agreed after the death of Nicholas the goods and implements of the farm shall belong to Benoni"

Dated, Dec 9, 1678

York deeds, Vol 3, p 41

"Nicholas Hodgsden of Kittery for £130 sells his son Benoni all that my mansion or dwelling house and all barnes and edifices All of which I heretofore purchased of John Wincoll, containing 40 acres Also 56 acres of land long since Granted unto me by the town of Kittery, Bounded by the great River Pischataqua, or at least a branch thereof on the West, and with a fresh brook on ye North, which brooke devides between my lands and one Left Playstead's land, late deceased And on ye East with certain marked trees, and on the South with land of Miles Thompson ———except about seven acres given John Morrell and his wife Sarah

Benoni to provide for Nicholas and his wife Elizabeth Benoni to pay her £6 yearly during her natural life"

Dated, Oct 22, 1678

York deeds, Vol. 3, p. 31.

The seven acres given to John Morrell and his wife Sarah, were deeded them by Nicholas and his wife Elizabeth, Dec. 3, 1671. The lot was situated in the northeast corner of the homestead, and was bounded on the north by Birchen Point Brook. After being owned by various parties, the lot was purchased by Benoni Hodsdon in 1703, when the entire homestead was once more owned by one of the Hodsdon family, where it remained for the succeeding 125 years.

Nicholas Hodsdon m. about 1639, Esther Wines, a cousin of Faintnot Wines of Charlestown, as proved by the following.

Faintnot Wines, Flaxdresser, inhabitant of Charlestown, Mass., 1635, with wife Bridget. He d. Feb. 25, 1664, will dated Sept. 4, 1663, proved June 20, 1665. Devised legacies to five of Nicholas Hodgdon's children by his cousin Esther Wines. Wife Esther d. in Hingham, Mass., Nov. 29, 1647, and he m. (2) between May 25, 1648, and Oct. 2, 1650, Elizabeth, widow of John Needham, as proved by the following, from Aspinwall Notarial Records:

"25. 3. 1648, I did testifie unto a Lee of the Attorney made from Eliz. Needham to John Searlet to receive all such goods as were due or belonging to her husband in Virginia. She being credibly informed of his death." p. 128.

"2. 8. 1650, Nicholas Hodsdon and Eliz. his wife (formerly wife of John Needham) did make ordeine &c: Peter Brackett of Braintre in N. E, theire true & lawful Attorney to ask &c: of Capt. Varvell or any other in whose hands maybe certaine goods of her former husband John Needham, shipped aboard the shipp of the said Capt. Varvell to carry to Virginia, & of the receipt to give acquittance &c: also to compound &c: & to appear in any Court or Courts &c: & generally to doe all things &c: with power to substitute &c: ratifying &c:" p. 324.

The place and date of death of Nicholas and Elizabeth is unknown. They were probably buried in the graveyard which was laid out on a portion of the homestead, to which reference is made in the deed given May 17, 1828. "Reserving and excepting from this conveyance one eighth of an acre on the homestead first above mentioned, which has been heretofore used as a place of burial by our ancestors." Children:

2. Esther Hodsdon,[2] +
3. Mehitable Hodsdon,[2] +
4. Jeremiah Hodsdon,[2] +
5. Israel Hodsdon,[2] +
6. Elizabeth Hodsdon;[2] bapt. Hingham, July 19, 1646; d. young.
7. Benoni Hodsdon,[2] +
8. Sarah Hodsdon,[2] +
9. Timothy Hodsdon,[2] +
10. John Hodsdon,[2] +
11. Joseph Hodsdon,[2] +
12. Lucy Hodsdon,[2] +

ESTHER Hodsdon[2] (2), bapt. in Hingham, Mass., Sept. 20, 1640; m. in Dover, N. H., Dec. 25, 1663, Edward Weymouth (perhaps son of Robert of Kittery, who came from Dartmouth, Co. Devon, England as early, says Farmer; as 1652.) Edward b. 1639, was taxed in Dover in 1662. He had a grant in Kittery, Me., in 1671 and bought land in what is now the northern part of Eliot, Me., in 1672. Their house was burned by Indians in 1677, he was a tailor by trade and they were living in 1710. Children:

13. Timothy Weymouth,[3] +
14. Mehitable Weymouth, [3] +

MEHITABLE Hodsdon,[2] (3), bapt. in Hingham, Mass. Nov. 1641; m. in Salem, Mass., Nov. 3, 1665, Peter Welcome of Boston, Mass. They lived for a time in Salem then in Boston where she d. between 1673-81; and he m. (2) widow Mehitable Howard who had a dau. Mary Howard mentioned in Peter Welcome's will as his dau-in-law, giving her one half his dwelling house, shop, salt house, wharf, &c. She paying to his son (her half brother) Joseph Welcome now at sea thirty pounds on his coming of age. He also gives his dau. Mary Townsend the household furniture which he had before his marriage with widow Mehitable Howard, who had d. Oct. 23, 1694; his will was dated Feb. 23, and probated Mar. 28, 1695. His inventory £245.00.0. Children:

15. Peter Welcome,[3] b. 1666.
16. Mehitable Welcome,[3] b. 1667.
17. Mary Welcome,[3] +
18. Samuel Welcome,[3] b. Dec. 22, 1673, not mentioned in his father's will.

JEREMIAH Hodsdon,[2] (4), bapt. in Hingham, Mass., Sept. 6, 1643; moved with his father to Boston, Mass., and later to Kittery; Me., where he he had grant of land laid out to him in 1666, being about twenty acres which he afterwards sold to his brother Israel, as five years later James Emery and Richard Nason testified that they laid out to Jeremiah Hodgdon the land that Israel's house now stands on dated 1671. Kittery town records.

Jeremiah Hodsdon was taxed in Cochecho, (now Dover, N. H.,) 1666. He m. about 1666-7, Anne, dau. of Alexander and Anne Thwaits, he came in the Hopewell from London, in 1635, aged 20, he was first at Concord, leaving there in 1640, and we find him afterward in Maine owning land at the head of Casco Bay and then on the Kennebec River near Bath. His children were Elizabeth, Anne, John, Rebecca, Alexander, Lydia, Jonathan, Mary and Margaret Thwaits.

Jeremiah settled in Portsmouth, N. H., and later at Great Island (now Newcastle); he died before 1716, and his widow afterward lived in Boston where she joined the Brattle Street Church, June 7, 1719. She and her sister Mary, wife of Edward Gilling, sell land once belonging to their father lying in Maine on the Kennebec river Mar. 5, 1724; and in said deed it is stated that five of her father's children are dead leaving no heirs. Children:

19. Alexander Hodgdon,[3] +
20. John Hodgdon,[3] +
21. Elizabeth Hodgdon,[3] +
22. Nathaniel Hodgdon,[3] +
23. Rebecca Hodgdon,[3] +

ISRAEL Hodsdon[2] (5), bapt at Hingham, Mass, July 19, 1646, moved with his father to Boston, and later to Kittery, Me., m about 1670, Ann, dau of Miles and Ann (Tetherly) Thompson of Kittery The first record concerning Israel Hodsdon in Kittery is the following land grant

"Laid out unto Israel Hodgdon, his grant of ten or twelve acres, at ye east end of his house lot, Eightie rods in length to a great white oak, bounded on ye North with Etherington's land and on ye East with land of William Gowen, and on ye South with land of Tristram Harrison"

Dated, Mar. 2, 1671

Kittery town records

Also "James Emery and Richard Nason testified that five years ago they laid out to Jeremiah Hodgdon, the land that Israel's house now stands on, being about twenty acres, bounded on the North by Ethrington's land and ye Commons on ye East"

Dated, 1671

Kittery town records

And "Laid out to Daniel Emery twenty-two acres and half of land it being part of a grant of 40 acres that was given to Israel Hodgdon by the town of Kittery Apr 13, 1671"

Dated, 1722

Kittery town records

The last mention we find of Israel Hodsdon is the following "Miles Thompson and wife, James Heard and wife, Nicholas Hodsdin and wife, Thomas Spencer and wife, William Furbush and wife, Israel Hodsden and wife and Richard Nason and wife were presented for not attending meeting"

Jul 6, 1675

York county Court records

It would look as though Israel Hodsdon and his father as well as some of their neighbors favored the Quakers, who were not popular at that time, for we find Nov 12, 1659, in company with John Heard of Kittery, Nicholas was ordered to appear at the second session of the General Court, to be held at Boston, and answer to the charge of entertaining Quakers To this Nicholas plead not guilty, but it was ordered that he be admonished by the Governor.

We do not find the date of Israel Hodsden's death, but his widow m. (2) about 1675-6, Robert Evans of Dover, N. H. He had had former wife, Elizabeth, dau. of Edward and Ann (———) Colcord of Hampton, N. H. We do not find the death of Elizabeth, but her last child was b. Jan. 25, 1671-2, and the first child of Robert and Ann Evans was b. in 1676. Robert Evans d. in Dover, Feb. 27, 1697, and his widow Ann was bapt. in the first church in Dover, Oct. 30, 1720, and admitted a member of the church the following month. She d. about 1727, and administration on her estate was granted to her eldest son, Israel Hodsdon, May 30, 1727; in one of the papers in the case he mentions her as his mother. The children of Robert and Ann (Thompson-Hodsdon) Evans, b. in Dover, were:

1. Mary Evans, b. 1676; m. Samuel Hart.
2. Joseph Evans, b. June 4, 1682; m. Mercy Horn.
3. Sarah Evans, b. Nov. 9, 1685; m. William Lewis.
4. Benjamin Evans, b. Feb. 2, 1687; m. Mary ———.
5. Hannah Evans, b. June 21, 1690; m. Zachariah Field; m. (2) Richard Hussey; they were ancestors of John Greenleaf Whittier.
6. Patience Evans, b. Sept. 5, 1693; m. Samuel Searle.

The estate of Israel Hodsdon was not settled until after his only son, Israel Jr., came of age, as shown by the following:

"Administration is granted to Israel Hodsden of the estate of his deceased father Israel Hodsden, late of Kittery, in ye County of Yorke, and the said Israel Hodsden, as principal, Bartholomew Thompson and Thomas Thompson as sureties, own themselves to be holden and firmly obliged unto Samuel Wheelwright, Esq., his Successors in ye office of Judge of Probate, within the County of York, in the sum of seventy pounds. That the said Israel Hodsdon shall well and truly administer on the Estate of his deceased father Israel Hodsden, aforesaid, according to law."
Dated, Jan. 19, 1696.

York County Probate Records

"A true Inventory of all and Singular the goods, chattels and credits of Israel Hodsden, planter deceased, praised at Berwick this 19th of Jany 1696-7, as follows

Imp	The house lot with the addition	£25—00—00
	fifty acres of land, near ye third Hill	05—00—00
	that piece of land and meadow in partnership, Lying at the Heathy Marsh	08—00—00
	total	£38—00—00

Nathan Lord
Andrew Neals
Nicholas Gowen
Inventory returned, Apr 1697"
York County Probate records

Israel Hodsdon, as administrator of his father's estate, sold the entire to Daniel Emery by the following deed

"Israel Hodsden of Portsmouth sell Daniel Emery of Kittery, a piece or Parcel of land containing twelve acres situated in Kittery, bounded as follows on the North with Etherington's land, on ye East with William Gowen, on ye south with Tristram Harris, on ye West with land formerly laid out to Jeremiah Hodgdon, together with fifty acres in Kittery, near the Third Hill, bounded East by Edward Weymouth, South by William Gowens and John Breadens, West with ye Common and North by Stephen Jenkins"
Dated, Feb 7, 1697
York deeds, Vol 4, p 98

Israel Hodsdon seems to have d in 1675, as his widow m (2) early in 1676 Children.

24 Ann Hodsdon,[3] +
25 Israel Hodsdon,[3] +

BENONI Hodsdon[2] (7), bapt in Hingham, Mass, Dec 5, 1647 (after the death of his mother) Moved with his father to Boston and later to Kittery, Me, where he m Abigail, dau of Thomas Curtis of Scituate, Mass, and York, Me He lived first at Quamphegon, near Salmon Falls, N. H., where his house was burned by the Indians, Oct, 16, 1675, and a number of the inhabitants slain. He was given the homestead at Birchen Point, Kittery, by his father Oct. 22, 1678. He was a prominent man in Kittery (now Berwick, Me.,); selectman in 1692 and 1694; was also an influential member of the church, and one of the committee to locate the meeting house in 1701, also representative in 1718. Benoni sold his homestead Mar. 2, 1713, to his son Thomas, he to pay his brothers and sisters a certain sum as their share of their father's estate. He d. in 1718, and administration on his estate was granted to his widow, May 15, 1718. Children:

26. Joseph Hodsdon,[3] +
27. Samuel Hodsdon,[3] +
28. Thomas Hodsdon,[3] +
29. Hannah Hodsdon,[3] +
30. Abigail Hodsdon,[3] +
31. John Hodsdon,[3] +
32. Esther Hodsdon,[3] +
33. Elizabeth Hodsden,[3] +

SARAH Hodsdon[2] (8), b. in Boston or vicinity about 1650; m. before 1674, John Morrell, who was b. in 1640 (as shown in a deposition). He had a grant of land in 1668-9. Dec. 3, 1674, Nicholas Hodsdon gave his daughter Sarah and her husband, John Morrell, seven acres of land adjoining the homestead at Birchen Point Brook. He was a mason by trade, and in 1676 he settled at "Cold Harbor," now Eliot, Me. He was licensed to keep a ferry and house of entertainment in 1686; was living in 1720. Children:

34. Nicholas Morrell,[3] +
35. Sarah Morrell,[3] +
36. John Morrell,[3] +
37. Adah Morrell,[3] +
38. Hannah Morrell,[3] +
39. Abraham Morrell,[3] +
40. Elizabeth Morrell,[3] +

TIMOTHY Hodsdon[2] (9), b in Boston, Mass, or Kittery, Me, about 1652, m Hannah ——— Nicholas Hodsdon sold his son Timothy land in Kittery, adjoining that of John Morrell, in 1679, this lot Timothy sold to his brother Benoni, Apr 3, 1682, and settled in York, Me, where he d about 1719, and his widow m Joseph Smith of York Children

41 Hannah Hodsdon,[3] +
42 William Hodsdon,[3] +
43 Sarah Hodsdon,[3] +

JOHN Hodsdon[2] (10), b in Boston, Mass, or Kittery, Me, in 1654, m Rebecca ——— He was a seafaring man and plied his vocation along the coast and on the several rivers in the vicinity of Kittery Nov 22, 1734, a quitclaim deed was given him by the heirs of Nicholas Hodsdon, in which reference is made to a deed given him some years previous by his brothers and sisters, and which deed has been lost, in this last deed, the descendants of Nicholas Hodsdon sell all their right, title and interest to a grant of 100 acres, which was given Nicholas by the town of Kittery, June 24, 1673 No date of death, last mentioned in 1734

JOSEPH Hodsdon[2] (11), b in Kittery, Me, 1656, m Tabitha, dau of Francis and Elinor (———) Raynes of York Me He was granted twenty acres of land at Nonesuch Point, in Falmouth, (now Portland) Mar 16, 1681-2 About 1687, he sold land in Falmouth and settled in York, where he d in 1691 The inventory of his estate was filed June 9, 1691, by his brother John Hodsdon Francis Raynes by his will dated July 28, 1698, gave Francis and Elizabeth Hodsdon, children of the late Joseph Hodsdon, certain legacies Children

44 Francis Hodsdon,[3]
45 Elizabeth Hodsdon,[3]

LUCY Hodsdon[2] (12), b probably in Kittery, Me, about 1660, m in 1681-2, George, son of George and Rebecca (Phipney) Vick-

ers or Vickery of Hull, Mass. July 24, 1721, she gave a dee
her brother, John Hodsdon, in which she sold all her right,
grant of 100 acres of land, which was granted to their fat
Nicholas Hodsdon. They lived for a time in Boston, Mass.,
then in Hull. We have not the date of his death, but she
widow at the home of her son-in-law Joseph Lewis, Dec. 25, 1
in Hingham, Mass. Children:

46. Sylvanus Vickers,[3] +
47. Hannah Vickers,[3] +
48. George Vickers,[3] +
49. Elizabeth Vickers,[3] +
50. Lucy Vickers,[3] b. Oct. 20, 1695. d. Aug. 2, 1698.
51. Israel Vickers,[3] b. Nov. 30, 1698; d. Jan. 28, 1699.
52. Israel Vickers,[3] +

TIMOTHY Weymouth[3] (13), b. in Dover, N. H., or Kitt
Me., 1664-5; m. (1) Rachel ———, who d. soon; m. (2) Patie
dau. of Daniel and Patience (Goodwin) Stone, b. in Kittery, M
23, 1683. He was living in 1759, in Kittery; she d. Apr.
1768. Children:

53. Rachel Weymouth,[4] +
54. Ichabod Weymouth,[4] +
54 a. Shadrach Weymouth,[4] +
54 b. Patience Weymouth,[4] b. Mar. 10, 1712; m. 1738, Rol
Morrell,[3] (160).
54 c. Sarah Weymouth,[4] b. Aug. 27, 1714.
54 d. Timothy Weymouth,[4] +
54 e. Jonathan Weymouth,[4] b. June 16, 1723.
54 f. Mary Weymouth,[4] b. Oct. 30, 1727.

MEHITABLE Weymouth[3] (14), b. in Kittery, Me., C.
1669; m. William, son of Thomas and Susan (Wooster) Stacy
in Ipswich, Mass., Apr. 21, 1656. They lived in Kittery, n
of Sturgeon Creek. She was appointed administrator of his
tate Mar. 5, 1706; she d. in 1753. Children:

55 Mary Stacy,[4] +
56 Hester Stacy,[4] b Nov 22, 1693
57 William Stacy, Jr,[4] b Jan 12 1696, living in 1754
58 Samuel Stacy,[4] +
59 Elizabeth Stacy,[4] b Aug 10, 1701
60 Benjamin Stacy,[4] +
61 Mehitable Stacy,[4] +

MARY Welcome[3] (17). b in Salem, Mass, about 1670, m in Boston, Mass, Nov 15, 1694, Peter, son of Peter and Lydia Townsend, b in Boston, Oct 9, 1671 They lived in Boston Children

62 Mary Townsend,[4] +
63 Peter Townsend,[4] +
64 Mehitable Townsend,[4] +
65 William Townsend,[4] +
66 Sarah Townsend,[4]

ALEXANDER Hodgdon[3] (19), b probably at Portsmouth, N H, m Jane Shackford of Dover, N H, and we first find mention of them in 1713, when he was member of a committee to obtain the services of a minister to settle in Newington, N H, where his wife, Jane, owned the covenant and was baptized Aug 6, 1727 Alexander Hodgdon, of Newington, sold land in Newinton, to his son-in-law John Grow of Newington, Feb 6, 1748-9, also Oct 13, 1752, to same party May 15, 1753, he sells to his son Alexander, Jr, of Rochester, N H, for £1600 00 0 all the land in Newington he then owned, being the home place We find nothing later in regard to him Children

67 Alexander Hodgdon,[4] +
68 Joseph Hodgdon,[4] +
69. John Hodgdon,[4] +
70 Benjamin Hodgdon,[4] +
71 Ann Hodgdon,[4] +
72 Elizabeth Hodgdon,[4] bapt in Newington, Oct 7, 1716

JOHN Hodgdon[3] (20), b. in Portsmouth, N. H., or Newington, N. H., m. Mary Hoyt (?). (We find on the vital records in Boston, Mass., the marriage of John Hodgdon and Susanna Clapp of Dorchester, Mass., May 5, 1702; this seems to have been a mistake in the name of the bridegroom, as we find Susanna the wife of Nathaniel Hodgdon in 1703, also her birth in Dorchester, and death and age from "Copp's Hill Epitaphs." John and Mary lived in Newington, where he signed a petition in 1713 for the settling of a minister in Newington. We find them selling land in 1729-35, to John Knight, John then a blacksmith. Feb. 18, 1736, Mary, widow of John Hodgdon, sell land in Newington to the same party. Children:

73. Jeremiah Hodgdon,[4] +
74. John Hodgdon, Jr.,[4] +

ELIZABETH Hodgdon[3] (21) b. in Portsmouth, N. H., or Newington, N. H.; m. (1) Benjamin Galloway; m. (2) in Dover, N. H., Nov. 19, 1702, Benjamin Richards. Alexander and John Hodgdon sell land in Newington, formerly belonging to their father, Jeremiah Hodgdon, with Benjamin Richards, who had married one of their sisters.

NATHANIEL Hodgdon[3] (22), b. in Portsmouth, N. H. (?), 1681; m. May 5, 1702, Susanna, dau. of Hopestill and Susanna (Swift) Clapp, b. in Dorchester, Mass., Dec. 23, 1673; is mentioned in her father's will, Sept. 2, 1719. She d. May 23, 1730, aged 56. He m. (2) Nov. 26, 1730, Ann, dau. of John and Mary (Lang-Smith) Atwood of Boston, Mass.; she d. June 9, 1748, aged 51; he m. (3) Dec. 1, 1748, Sarah Porter, who is mentioned in his will. Nathaniel was a leather dresser in Boston, and served as a clerk of the market, 1720; sealer of leather, 1725 and 1731-54, inclusive (except 1733-4 and 1738); was first sergeant of the artillery company, 1728. He d. Dec. 6, 1757. Children:

75. Tabitha Hodgdon,[4] +
76. Joseph Hodgdon,[4] b. June 5, d. Aug. 17, 1704.
77. Susannah Hodgdon,[4] +

78 Patience Hodgdon,[4] +
79 Elizabeth Hodgdon,[4] +
80 Mary Hodgdon,[4] bapt Jan 21, 1711, d young
81 Ann Hodgdon,[4] b Sept 29, 1731, d May 18, 1733
82 Mary Hodgdon,[4] b Nov 19, 1733
83 Tabitha Hodgdon,[4] bapt Nov 2, 1735, d young
84 Ann Hodgdon,[4] bapt Mar 6, 1737
85 Tabitha Hodgdon [4] bapt June 17, 1739

REBECCA Hodgdon[3] (23), b in Portsmouth, N H, or Newington, N H, m in Boston, Mass, July 9, 1707, Edward Bedford

ANN Hodgdon[3] (24), b in Kittery, Me, about 1671-2, m about 1690, John, son of John and Mary (Nutter) Wingate, and grandson of Hatevil and Mary Nutter of Dover, N H He was b in Dover July 13, 1670, d in 1715 She m (2) Dec, 1725, Capt John, son of James and Shuah Heard, she was living in 1727 His will was dated Jan 15, 1739 Children

86 Mary Wingate,[4] b in Dover, Oct 3, 1691, m Josiah Clark.
87 John Wingate,[4] +
88 Ann Wingate,[4] +
89 Sarah Wingate,[4] +
90 Moses Wingate,[4] +
91 Samuel Wingate,[4] b Nov 27, 1700, m Mrs Mary (Roberts) Heard
92 Edmund Wingate,[4] b Feb 27, 1702
93 Abigail Wingate,[4] b Mar 2, 1704
94 Elizabeth Wingate,[4] b Feb 3, 1706, m John Hodsdon,[3] (31)
95 Mehitable Wingate,[4] b Nov 14, 1709
96 Joanna Wingate,[4] b Jan 6, 1711; m Ebenezer Hill
97 Simon Wingate,[4] b Sept 2, 1713, m Lydia Hill

ISRAEL Hodgdon[3] (25), b in Kittery, Me, 1673-4, little has been found concerning his early life, his father died when he was an infant, and his mother married a second time. We think he may have lived with his uncle Jeremiah as we find him at Portsmouth, N.H., in 1696, when he was appointed administrator of his father's estate On Apr. 7, 1696, the town of Dover, N.H., gave him a grant of land. He probably m. before this time, Ann Wingate, sister of John Wingate who had m. his sister Ann; she was b. in Dover, Feb. 18, 1667, and was living in 1740. They lived in Dover, and in the several deeds he gave he is called a "housewright" or carpenter.

June 15, 1702. "Israel Hodgdon and Ann his wife, sell John Drew, Sen., of Dover, a parcel of land containing twenty acres, which land was granted by ye Town of Dover to my father-in-law, John Winget in the year 1658. Situated on the West side of the Back River, bordering on the North by a twenty acre lot granted at the same time to John Roberts and lays between Roberts' lot and a twenty acre lot granted to Ralph Hall."

(N. H. Deeds, vol. 6, p. 328.)

The date of his death has not been found, except through the date of making and probating his will.

Will of Israel Hodgdon of Dover, Dated Jan. 21, 1739-40.

"I give to my loving wife Ann Hodgdon, all my quick stock as oxen, cows, young cattle, horses, sheep, swine, and also all my household goods, that is to say, besides bedding of every kind and all the utensils to the house belonging.

"I give and bequeath to my son Israel Hodgdon, twenty acres of land, being part of my right in the Division of the Common Land. Israel Hodgdon Paying to his brother, Moses Hodgdon of Berwick, twenty pounds, within six months after my decease.

"I give and bequeath unto my son Shadrach Hodgdon, ten acres of land, being part of my right in the Division of the Commons.

"I give and bequeath unto my three sons, Israel Hodgdon, Moses Hodgdon, and Shadrach Hodgdon, all my Ox Tackling, as Yokes, Chains and Wheels and such things as belong there unto, to be equally divided between them, and also my clothes to divided between the said three sons.

"I give and bequeath to my two daughters, Mary Randall and Abigail Ham, all that part of the moveable Estate that shall remain at my wife's decease, to be equally divided between them, and I do hereby make and appoint my loving wife Ann Hodgdon, full and sole Executor of this my last Will and Testament, hereby revoking, Disannulling and making void, all former Wills and bequests by me made and declaring this only to be my last Will and Testament

Witnessed by Richard Clark
Robert Evans ISRAEL HODGDON"

Probated, Jan 30, 1750

Children

98 Israel Hodgdon, Jr,[4] +
99 Moses Hodgdon,[4] +
100. Shadrach Hodgdon,[4] +
101 Abigail Hodgdon,[4] m Ebenezer Ham
102 Mary Hodgdon,[4] +

JOSEPH Hodsdon[3] (26), b in Kittery, Me, ——, m about 1699, Margaret, dau of Daniel, Jr, and Amy (Thompson) Goodwin, b in Kittery, Aug. 23, 1683 They lived in Berwick, Me, where his will was probated, Apr 4, 1764 Children

103 Abigail Hodsdon,[4] +
104 Benjamin Hodsdon,[4] +
105 Annie or Amy Hodsdon,[4] +
106 Joseph Hodsdon,[4] bapt Apr 19, 1716, (with his four sisters) living in 1756
107. Margaret Hodsdon,[4] +
108 Elizabeth Hodsdon,[4] +
109 Judith Hodsdon,[4] bapt Apr 19, 1716, unm in 1756
110 Sarah Hodsdon,[4] bapt Apr 19, 1716, m —— Lewis
111 Prudence Hodsdon,[4] bapt July 17, 1720, living in 1774, unm

SAMUEL Hodsdon[3] (27), b in Kittery, Me, m ——about 1722, Prudence, dau of Richard and Elizabeth (Wakely) Scammon who was b. about 1700. They were both bapt. at Sout Berwick, Me., Sept. 3, 1722, and their children were also bap there. His estate was administered in 1755. Children:

112. Abigail Hodsdon,[4] +
113. Daniel Hodsdon,[4] +
114. Prudence Hodsdon,[4] bapt. May 11, 1729, d. young.
115. Thomas Hodsdon,[4] +
116. Prudence Hodsdon,[4] +
117. Scammon Hodsdon,[4] bapt. Oct. 26, 1741; living in 175(
118. Samuel Hodsdon,[4] living in 1756.
119. Richard Hodsdon,[4] +
120. Benjamin Hodsdon,[4]
121. Elizabeth Hodsdon,[4] m. Daniel Furbush, Jr.
122. Sarah Hodsdon,[4] +

THOMAS Hodsdon[3] (28), b. in Kittery, Me; —— —m. Dec 1, 1709, Mary, dau. of Nathan Jr., and Martha (Tozier) Lord b in Kittery, July 29, 1691. He d. before May, 1717. She m. (2 June 16, 1720, Daniel Emery, Jr. Children:

123. Anna Hodsdon,[4] bapt. July 26, 1713.
124. John Hodsdon,[4] +
125. Mary Hodsdon,[4] +

HANNAH Hodsdon[3] (29), b. in Kittery, Me., ———; m Nov. 17, 1709, Richard Shackley of Berwick, Me.; they lived i the southern part of the town. His will was dated Feb. 27, 1783 probated, Mar. 1, 1783-4. Children:

126. Samuel Shackley,[4] b. Nov. 2, d. Dec. 21, 1710.
127. Mary Shackley,[4] +
128. Hannah Shackley,[4] b. Apr. 21, 1713; m. ——— Kimball
129. Richard Shackley, Jr.,[4] +
130. Miriam Shackley,[4] +
131. Abigail Shackley,[4] +
132. Samuel Shackley,[4] +
133. John Shackley,[4] +

134 Elizabeth Shackley,[4] +
135 Sarah Shackley,[4] +

ABIGAIL Hodsdon[3] (30), b in Kittery, Me, 1664, m in 1694, Nicholas, son of William and Elizabeth (Frost) Gowen (sometimes called Smith, because the word Gowan means a smith, or work in Scotland) Nicholas served in his younger days as an Indian scout, but later studied law and was admitted to practice as an attorney at a court held in York, Apr 6, 1703 Was representative to General Court in 1709, and d about 1742 Children:

136 Abigail Gowen,[4] +
137 Elizabeth Gowen,[4] +
138 Margaret Gowen,[4] +
139. Hester Gowen,[4] +
140 Nicholas Gowen,[4] b Nov 12, 1703
141 William Gowen,[4] +
142 Patrick Gowen,[4] b Mar 30, 1707, m Miriam Shackley[4] (130)
143 Anna Gowen,[4] +
144 James Gowen,[4] +

JOHN Hodsdon[3] (31), bapt in Boston, Mass, (his mother being of the church in Berwick, Me,) July 24, 1698, m Elizabeth,[4] dau of John and Ann (Hodsdon) Wingate, (94) b in Dover, N H, Feb 3, 1706 He d before 1733 Children

145 John Hodsdon,[4] +
146 Stephen Hodsdon,[4] +

ESTHER Hodsdon[3] (32), b in Berwick, Me, ——— m about 1720, Thomas Horn of Dover, N H Children

147 Judith Horn,[4] +
148 Margaret Horn,[4] b Apr 16, 1722
149 Samuel Horn,[4] b Feb 16, 1724
150 Abigail Horn,[4] b Dec 7, 1725
151. Drusilla Horn,[4] b June 18, 1727.

152. Esther Horn,[4] b. Apr. 26, 1729.
153. Nathan Horn,[4] bapt. Oct. 13, 1734.
154. Elizabeth Horn,[4] bapt. Oct. 13, 1734, with their brothers and sisters
155. Paul Horn,[4] b. Sept. 5, 1737.

ELIZABETH Hodsdon[3] (33), b. in Berwick, Me; ——— m. James, son of Daniel and Mary——— Ferguson, b. in 1676 They were both slain by Indians Sept. 28, 1707. Child:

156. James Ferguson,[4] +

NICHOLAS Morrell[3] (34), b. in Kittery, or Eliot, Me., 1667 (as shown in a deposition); m. in 1695, Sarah, dau. of Abraham and Sarah (White) Frye. He was a blacksmith; his estate was administered in 1757. Children:

157. Sarah Morrell,[4] +
158. Elizabeth Morrell,[4] b. Mar. 18, 1698; m. Dec. 2, 1721, Thomas Hobbs.
159. John Morrell,[4] +
160. Robert Morrell,[4] +
161. Anne Morrell,[4] b. Dec. 1, 1708; m. Sept 2, 1728, John Hall of Dover, N. H.

SARAH Morrell[3] (35), b. in Kittery, or Eliot, Me., ———; m. (1) Aug. 4, 1701, George Huntress of Dover, N. H. She m. (2) Thomas Darling.

JOHN Morrell[3] (36), b. in Kittery, or Eliot, Me, ———; m. Dec. 16, 1701, Hannah, dau. of Peter and Mary (Remick) Dixon, b. in Kittery, Feb. 3, 1684. He made his will in 1756, probated in 1763. She d. Dec. 20, 1765. Children:

162. John Morrell,[4] +
163. Thomas Morrell,[4] b. Aug. 20, 1705; not mentioned in his father's will.
164. Peter Morrell,[4] +

165 Jedediah Morrell,[4] +
166 Richard Morrell,[4] b Sept 23, 1713, not mentioned in his father's will
167 Keziah Morrell,[4] m ——— Roberts.
168 Mary Morrell,[4] +

ADAH Morrell[3] (37), b in Kittery, or Eliot, Me, m Apr 27, 1702, Jonathan, son of Jonathan and Sarah (Jenkins) Nason, both were bapt at Berwick, Me., and owned the covenant Apr 13, 1712 His will dated Nov 4, 1745, probated, Apr 7, 1746, his wife was then living Children

169 Richard Nason,[4] +
170 John Nason,[4] +
171 Mary Nason,[4] +
172 Sarah Nason,[4] +
173 Jonathan Nason,[4] b Nov 7, 1710, living in 1745
174 Uriah Nason,[4] +
175 Adah Nason,[4] +
176 Azariah Nason,[4] +
177 Philadelphia Nason,[4] +
178 Rachel Nason,[4] b May 1, 1724, d young
179 Elizabeth Nason,[4] +

HANNAH Morrell[3] (38), b in Kittery, or Eliot, Me, ———, m about 1712, John, son of Robert and Sarah (Libby) Tidy, he d Jan, 1766 Children

180 Sarah Tidy,[4] m June, 1738, Benjamin Stacy[4] (60)
181 Adah Tidy,[4] +
182 Hannah Tidy,[4] b July 6, 1718, d about 1799, when the name of Tidy became extinct
183 Robert Tidy,[4] b Oct. 12, 1720, published May 14, 1743, with Hannah Goold He d before 1790, leaving no family
184 Meribah Tidy,[4] b Sept 12, 1722, d
185 John Tidy, b June 29, 1724, d 1749, unm

ABRAHAM Morrell[3] (39), b in Kittery, or Eliot, Me, ———, m Phebe, dau of Capt John and Phebe (Littlefield) Heard, b in Kittery, Jan 15, 1692, he d soon and she m (2) 1724, Thomas Stevens of Newcastle, N H

ELIZABETH Morrell[3] (40), b in Kittery, or Eliot, Me, ———, m in Boston, Mass, Feb 3, 1698, Samuel, son of Leonard and Elizabeth (Abbott) Drowne, b in Kittery, Mar 7, 1676-7 He d Jan 25, 1720-1, as his headstone on the old Morrell homestead showed Children

186 Elizabeth Drowne,[4] +
187 Samuel Drowne,[4] +
188 Solomon Drowne,[4] b Mar 26, 1706, in Boston
189 Thomas Drowne,[4] b Dec 23, 1708, in Boston

HANNAH Hodsdon[3] (41), b in York, Me, ———; m June 25, 1695, Nicholas Smith

WILLIAM Hodgdon[3] (42), b in Kittery, or York, Me, ———, m in Dorchester, Mass, June 12, 1713, Mary Eames of Dorchester She d and he m (2) Margery ———, they lived in Barnstable, Mass Child

190 Timothy Hodgdon,[4] b in Boston, Mass, Nov 25, 1725

SARAH Hodsdon[3] (43), b in Kittery, or York, Me, ———, m Samuel Cox of Boston, Mass

SYLVANUS Vickers[3] (46), b in Hull, Mass, June 13, 1683, m in Boston, Mass, Nov 22, 1705, Mary Stiles, she d and he m (2) Dec 11, 1718, Anne Newell He was a blockmaker, his will was written June 24, 1721, giving everything to his wife Anne

HANNAH Vickers[3] (47), b in Hull, Mass, Sept 9, 1685, m May 23, 1704, John Lobdell

GEORGE Vickers[3] (48), b in Hull, Mass, Aug 14, 1688, m

Dec 10, 1710, Elizabeth, dau of John and Mercy Binney, b in Hull, Dec 3, 1690 Children

191 Mercy Vickers,[4] +
192 George Vickers,[4] +

ELIZABETH Vickers[3] (49), b in Hull, Mass, ——, m (1) in 1714, Dr John Dixon They lived in Hingham, Mass, where he was a practicing physician, he d Feb 14, 1717, aged 36, she m (2) July 16, 1718, Joseph, son of James and Sarah (Lane) Lewis, b in Barnstable, Mass, July, 1676 He was grandson of George and Sarah (Jenkins) Lewis, who came from East Greenwich, Kent, England According to Dean's History, dismissed from Plymouth Church in 1634, "in case they join in a body at Scituate" Joseph had had a former wife and seven children They lived in Hingham, where Elizabeth d Sept 1, 1736 He was selectman in 1718, and called a "hadder", he d Aug 22, 1767 Children

193 David Dixon,[4] b July 28, 1715
194 Daniel Dixon,[4] b Oct. 21, 1716, d 1718
195 Elizabeth Lewis,[4] +
196. George Lewis,[4] +
197 Hannah Lewis,[4] b May 24, d. Aug. 17, 1723
198 Samuel Lewis,[4] b June 28, d Aug 17, 1724
199 Samuel Lewis,[4] +
200 Israel Lewis,[4] b Apr 19, d July 30, 1727
201 Ebenezer Lewis,[4] +
202 Lucy Lewis,[4] b Oct 23, 1730, d. Feb 3, 1794
203 Hannah Lewis,[4] +
204 Eunice Lewis,[4] b May 9, 1736, d Sept 17, 1744

ISRAEL Vickers[3] (52), b in Hull, Mass, Dec 17, 1699, m. in Hingham, Mass, Dec 7, 1721, Lydia, dau of John and Mary (Warren) Burr b in Hingham, Aug 17, 1701 They lived in Hingham where he was drowned in the town cove, "near Col Thaxter's wharf," Nov 25, 1739, aged 40 She m (2) June 12, 1748, Henry Smith of Rehoboth, Mass Children

205 Lydia Vickers,[4] +
206 Hannah Vickers,[4] bapt Dec 12, 1726, d Feb 24, 1763
207 Deborah Vickers,[4] bapt Nov 5, 1730
208 Benjamin Vickers,[4] bapt Apr 27, 1733
209 An infant,[4] d Mar 11, 1738-9

RACHEL Weymouth[4] (53), b in Kittery, Me, Aug 10, 1705, m Oct 15, 1727, Isaac Powers

ICHABOD Weymouth[4] (54), b in Kittery, Me, Nov 23, 1707, m in 1736, Mary Knight of Berwick, Me, he d Dec 8, 1760,

SHADRACH Weymouth[4] (54a), b in Kittery, Me, Jan 4, 1709, published Mar 5, 1736, with Patience, dau of Gabriel and Mary———Hamilton, bapt in Berwick, Me, Sept 6, 1713 She d and he m (2) Winniford in 1737 He m (3) Elizabeth Knight Oct 24, 1746 Child

210 Pierce Weymouth,[5] bapt in Eliot, Me, Mar 1737

TIMOTHY Weymouth[4] (54 d), b in Kittery, Me, May 22, 1719, m Elizabeth, dau of Phillip and Elizabeth (Roberts) Hubbard, bapt in Berwick, Me, Nov 21, 1723 They lived in Kittery and Eliot, Me, where she d Feb 17, 1762, he d Feb 4, 1765 Children

211 Elizabeth Weymouth,[5] bapt in Eliot, May 1, 1748
212 Dorcas Weymouth,[5] bapt in Eliot, Nov 7, 1755
213 Jonathan Weymouth,[5] bapt in Eliot, Aug 4, 1758
214. Timothy Weymouth,[5] bapt in Weymouth, Sept 7, 1763

MARY Stacy[4] (55), b in Kittery, Me, Apr 6, 1990, m June 22, 1709, John, son of John and Sarah (Emery) Thompson They joined the church at South Berwick, Me, Sept 2, 1712, Mar 24, 1738-9, he sold 15 of 30 acres granted to Gilbert Warren (his step-father), "which grant I bought of my mother Sarah Warren" York deeds, XXXI 27 They lived in South Berwick and both d before 1754 Children

215 Esther Thompson,[5] b June 11, 1710
216 John Thompson,[5] +
217 Noah Thompson,[5] +
218 Sarah Thompson,[5] +
219 Ebenezer Thompson,[5] bapt Sept 9, 1716
220 Thomas Thompson,[5] bapt Sept 9, 1716
221 William Thompson,[5] bapt July 20, 1718
222 Amos Thompson,[5] bapt Mar 20, 1720.
223 Mary Thompson,[5] +
224 Miles Thompson,[5] bapt Apr 18, 1725

SAMUEL Stacy[4] (58), b in Kittery, Me, Apr 19, 1698, m Nov. 2, 1721, Mary, dau of Samuel and Mary (Fernald) Pray. She d in 1789 Children:

225 William Stacy,[5] +
226 Samuel Stacy,[5] b Jan 31, 1724-5
227 John Stacy,[5] b Jan 21, 1726-7
228 Ebenezer Stacy,[5] +
229 Benjamin Stacy,[5] b Apr 26, 1731
230 Timothy Stacy,[5] b May 31, 1733

BENJAMIN Stacy[4] (60), b in Kittery, Me, Nov 17, 1704; m (1) Oct 7, 1730, Lydia, dau of Mathew and Elizabeth (Brown) Libby, b in Kittery, Apr 27, 1713, she d and he m (2) June, 1738, Sarah[4] (180), dau of John and Hannah (Morrell[3]) Tidy, b in Kittery, Jan 17, 1713-4 He d Dec 25, 1758 Children

231 Ichabod Stacy,[5] b in 1731; m May 24, 1756, Lydia Guptill
232 Benjamin Stacy,[5] b in 1743, d 1768
233 Hannah Stacy,[5] +
234 Lydia Stacy,[5] +

MEHITABLE Stacy[4] (61), b in Kittery, Me, Apr 4, 1706, m Oct 10, 1726, Joseph, son of Job and Charity (Nason) Emery, b in South Berwick, Me, Feb 24, 1702, she d in 1786, he d July 1, 1793 Children:

235 James Emery,[6] +

236 John Emery,[6] +

237 Mary Emery,[5] b Nov 5, 1732

238 Esther Emery,[5] b May 31, 1731, m Asa Burbank

239 Mehitable Emery,[5] +

240 Stephen Emery,[6] b Mar 21, 1738

241 Elizabeth Emery,[5] b Feb 28, 1740

242 Joseph Emery,[6] b Aug 25, 1742, m Oct 30, 1767, Rebecca Wakefield

243 Job Emery,[5] b Jan 29, 1745; m Mary, dau of Joseph and Sarah (Emery) Hubbard, b Jan 12, 1745, she d Feb 24, 1812

244 William Emery,[5] b Feb 6, 1747, m Philomelia Webber

245 Josiah Emery,[5] b Sept 24, 1751

MARY Townsend[4] (62), b in Boston, Mass, about 1695, m in Boston, May 10, 1722, Joseph Prince They lived in Boston Children

246 Joseph Prince,[6] b Apr 12, 1723, m Jan 13, 1757, Mary Greenwood

247 Isaac Prince,[5] b Mar 26, 1725

248 Elizabeth Prince,[6] b Aug 13, 1727, d young

249 Caleb Prince,[5] b Oct 6, 1731, m Sept 25, 1755, Susanna Blake

250 James Prince,[5] b Jan 28, 1733-4

251 Elizabeth Prince,[5] } b Mar 2, 1736, m June 8, 1773, David Higgins

252 Abigail Prince,[6] } b Mar 2, 1736, m May 31 1762, Ebenezer Prout of Scarborough, Me

PETER Townsend[4] (63), b in Boston, Mass, 1697, m Mar 12, 1718, Mary Gilbert Child.

253 Mary Townsend,[6] b Jan 26, 1719

MEHITABLE Townsend[4] (64), b in Boston, Mass, bapt Feb 19, 1702, m Dec 28, 1723, Benjamin Salter

WILLIAM Townsend[4] (65), b in Boston, Mass, ———, m Nov 30, 1724, Hanna Golden, she d and he m. (2) before 2734, Mary ——— Children

254 William Townsend,[5] b. Sept. 28, 1734
255 Mary Townsend,[5] b Sept 8, 1738

ALEXANDER Hodgdon[4] (67), b in Portsmouth, or Newington, N H, about 1700, m about 1725, Mary Shackford The first mention we find of him is a deed of land in Barrington, N H, from Joshua Shackford, Nov 25, 1734, he soon settled in Rochester, N H, and we often find his name on deeds, the last being dated Jan 1, 1762, when he gives his son, Alexander, Jr, his home, reserving a life interest in it, no wife mentioned

Mar 1, 1762, Alexander Hodgdon of Rochester, sells to his son, Eleazer, of Dover, N H, land in Barrington and in Rochester We do not find his will or date of death Children:

256 Eleazer Hodgdon,[5] +
257 Samuel Hodgdon,[5] bapt in Newington, Sept 19, 1731
258 Ann Hodgdon,[5] +
259. Abigail Hodgdon,[5] bapt in Newington, June 11, 1734
260 Rebecca Hodgdon,[5] +
261 Alexander Hodgdon,[5] +

JOSEPH Hodgdon[4] (68), b in Portsmouth, or Newington, N H, ———m about 1719, Patience ———, they lived in Newington, where their children were baptized Children

262 Patience Hodgdon,[5] bapt May 15, 1720
263 Alexander Hodgdon,[5] bapt Oct 30, 1723
264 John Hodgdon,[5] bapt July 10, 1727
265 Patience Hodgdon,[5] bapt July 10, 1727
266 'Lydia Hodgdon,[5] bapt Dec 19, 1736
267 Abigail Hodgdon,[5] bapt Dec 19, 1736

JEREMIAH Hodgdon[4] (69), b in Portsmouth, or Newington, N H, m in Newington, Apr 16, 1721, Mary Babb He was bapt at the church in Newington, July 28, 1729, Aug 20, 1732 Jeremiah or Jeremy Hodgdon and wife Mary united with First church in Falmouth, now Portland, Me, and had three children baptized They remained in Falmouth, until 1740, which is the latest date we find of this family Children

268 James Hodgdon,[5] bapt in Falmouth, Aug 20, 1732
269 Benjamin Hodgdon,[5] bapt in Falmouth, Aug 20, 1732
270 Elizabeth Hodgdon,[5] bapt in Falmouth, Aug 20, 1732
271 Sarah Hodgdon,[5] bapt in Newington, Oct 3, 1731
272 Seth Hodgdon,[5] bapt in Famouth, Sept 17, 1732
273 Ann Hodgdon,[5] bapt in Falmouth, 1734
274 Jeremiah Hodgdon,[5] bapt in Falmouth, 1737
275 Mary Hodgdon,[5] bapt in Falmouth, 1740

JOHN Hodgdon[4] (70), b in Portsmouth, or Newington, N H, m about 1721-2, Mary ——— They lived in Newington, where they were bapt and united with the First Congregational Church, May 22, 1727 Children

276 Mary Hodgdon,[5] bapt in Newington, June 19, 1727
277 Mehitable Hodgdon,[5] bapt in Newington June 19, 1727
278 Elizabeth Hodgdon,[5] bapt in Newington, June 19, 1727
279 John Hodgdon,[5] bapt in Newington, Mar 3, 1728, d young
281 A child,[5] bapt Jan, 1736
284 John Hodgdon,[5] bapt in Newington, Jan 5, 1746

BENJAMIN Hodgdon[4] (72), b in Portsmouth, or Newington, N H, m in Boston, Mass, Oct 30, 1735, Rebecca Marshall They lived in Boston, where his will was written in 1772, proved June 18, 1773; in the settling of his estate he is said to be heir or have an interest in the property of Benjamin Stoakes, who m Nov 4, 1717, Rebecca Kerbee, and his daughter, Rebecca, who m Sept 18, 1739, John Montjoy. Children

287 Alexander Hodgdon,[5] +
288 Samuel Hodgdon,[5] a tailor in 1772

289 John Hodgdon [5]
290 Benjamin Hodgdon [5]
291 Rebecca Hodgdon,[5] +
292 William Hodgdon [5]
293 Joseph Hodgdon [5]

JOHN Hodgdon, Jr [4] (74), b in Newington, N H, m Jan 30, 1729, Mary Decker They lived in Newington, where his will was written Nov 2, 1782 probated July 17, 1793, granddaughter Hannah Pickering mentioned in his will Children

294 Jane Hodgdon,[5] m Coolbroth
295 Phineas Hodgdon,[5] +
296 Mary Hodgdon,[5] m Warren
297 Charles Hodgdon,[5] +
298 Temperance Hodgdon,[5] +
299 John Hodgdon, Jr,[5] +
300 Benjamin Hodgdon,[5] +
301 Sarah Hodgdon,[5] m in Newington, Sept 2, 1773, Stephen Ayers

TABITHA Hodgdon[4] (75) b in Boston, Mass, Jan 4, 1703; m Apr 2, 1723, in Boston, by Rev Cotton Mather, Thomas, son of Daniel and Elizabeth (Ballard) Stoddard They lived in Boston, where she d June 3, 1734, and was buried at Copp's Hill, he m (2) Abigail Barker, he d Apr 12, 1763 Children

302 Nathaniel Stoddard,[5] b in Boston, Apr 25, 1724
303 Elizabeth Stoddard,[5] +
304 Susannah Stoddard,[5] +
305 Thomas Stoddard,[5] b July 11, 1729, d young
306 Tabitha Stoddard,[5] b Sept 15, 1730
307 Sarah Stoddard,[5] +
308 Patience Stoddard,[5] +

ELIZABETH Hodgdon[4] (79), b in Boston, Mass, July 1, 1708, m in Boston, Jan 11, 1727, Joseph Lewis

JOHN Wingate[4] (87), b in Dover, N H, Apr 10, 1693, m in Dover, in 1717, Dorothy Tebbitts Children

309 John Wingate,[5] b May 5, 1719
310 Samuel Wingate,[5] b Feb 19, 1721
311 Daniel Wingate,[5] b Jan 28, 1722-3
312 Joshua Wingate,[5] b July 28, 1725
313 Jonathan Wingate,[5] bapt Oct 22, 1727
314 Moses Wingate,[5] bapt Nov 23, 1729
315 Elizabeth Wingate,[5] bapt Nov 23, 1729
316 Dorothy Wingate,[5] bapt Sept 23, 1733
317 Noah Wingate,[5] bapt Sept 27, 1735
318 Aaron Wingate,[5] bapt Feb 6, 1737
319 Sarah Wingate,[5] bapt Aug 20, 1738
320 Ann Wingate,[5] bapt Mar 14, 1742
321 Moses Wingate[5] } bapt Nov 28, 1743
322 Aaron Wingate,[5] }
323 Mehitable Wingate,[5] bapt. Feb 22, 1747

ANN Wingate[4] (88), b in Dover, N H, Feb 2, 1694, m in Dover, June 3, 1713, Francis Drew, he d May 10, 1717, and she m (2) Jan 1, 1719, Daniel Titcomb of Dover Children

324 Joseph Drew,[5] b Apr 8, 1717
325 Ann Titcomb,[5] b Oct 15, 1719
326 William Titcomb,[5] b Dec 20, 1721
327 Sarah Titcomb,[5] } b Jan 27, 1724
328 Mary Titcomb,[5] }
329 John Titcomb,[5] b Mar 20, 1727
330 Elizabeth Titcomb,[5] b Apr 21, 1728
331 Daniel Titcomb,[5] b Apr 30, 1731
332 David Titcomb,[5] b July 25, 1733
333 Abigail Titcomb,[5] bapt Nov 23, 1734
334 Enoch Titcomb,[5] bapt Apr 30, 1738
335 Benjamin Titcomb,[5] bapt June 12, 1743, m Dec 30, 1773, Hannah Hanson, he d of consumption, May 4, 1799, called Col Benjamin Titcomb

SARAH Wingate[4] (89), b in Dover, N H, Feb 17, 1696, m about 1716, Peter Hayes of Dover, where they lived Children

336 Ann Hayes,[5] b June 3, 1718
337 Reuben Hayes,[5] b May 8, 1720
338 Joseph Hayes,[5] b Mar 15, 1722
339 Benjamin Hayes,[5] b Mar 1, 1724
340 Mehitable Hayes,[5] b Mar 2, 1725
341 John Hayes,[5] bapt Oct 27, 1728
342 Lydia Hayes,[5] } bapt Apr 25, 1733 d young
343 Joanna Hayes,[5] }
344 Lydia Hayes,[5] bapt Aug 10, 1735
345 Ichabod Hayes,[5] bapt Oct 2, 1737
346 Elijah Hayes,[5] bapt Sept 27, 1741

MOSES Wingate[4] (90), b in Dover, N H, Dec 27, 1698, m about 1725, Abigail, dau of John and Mercy Church b in Dover, May 15, 1702 She united with the First Church in Dover, Sept 14, 1729, and had her two oldest children baptized Lieut Moses Wingate d in Dover, Feb 9, 1782, aged 84 Children

347 Edmund Wingate,[5] bapt with his mother, Sept 14, 1729
348 Abigail Wingate,[5] bapt with her mother, Sept 14, 1729
349 Deborah Wingate,[5] bapt Aug 2, 1730
350 Ebenezer Wingate,[5] bapt Mar 18, 1733
351 Ann Wingate,[5] bapt Oct 3, 1736
352 Moses Wingate,[5] bapt Aug 20, 1738
353 Benjamin Wingate,[5] bapt Sept 28, 1740
354 Ebenezer Wingate,[5] bapt May 23, 1742

ISRAEL Hodgdon, Jr (98), b in Dover, N H, Mar 25, 1697, m in Dover, Aug 9, 1725, Hannah, dau of John and Elizabeth (Meader) Hanson, b in Dover, Jan 11, 1705, they lived in Dover, where she d Jan 1, 1737-8 He m (2) in Dover, Sept 21, 1738, Mary, dau of Edmund and Abigail (Green) Johnson of Hampton, N H, b Nov 3, 1707

We find the following in the "Historical Memoranda Concerning Persons and Places in old Dover, N.H." "John Hanson was a son of Thomas Hanson, and grandson of Thomas, sen., who 'tooke the oeth of fidellitie' at Dover June 4, 1661. John lived at Nock's Marsh on the place where Samuel Hanson now lives. Being a Friend, he refused to leave his exposed position, and his house was marked for an attack. Thirteen Indians and French Mohawks, lay for several days near it in ambush, waiting until Hanson and his men were away, for the Indians were a cowardly set of villains; and when he had gone to the week-day meeting and two sons were at work at some distance, the Indians entered the house; Mrs. Hanson, a servant, and four children were in the house, of which, one child the Indians immediately killed to terrify the others; two other children were at play in the orchard, and would have escaped but that just as the Indians had finished rifling the house, the two came in sight and made such a noise that the Indians killed the youngest boy to stop an alarm, with Mrs. Hanson, her babe of two weeks, a boy of six years and two daughters, one fourteen years old, the other sixteen, and the servant girl. All reached Canada, but the party was repeatedly subdivided during the journey.

The first person who discoverd the tragedy was Hanson's oldest daughter (afterward Mrs. Hodgdon) on her return from meeting. Seeing the children dead she gave a shriek which was distinctly heard by her mother in the hands of the enemy and by her brothers at work. Persuit was instantly made but the Indians avoided all paths and escaped undiscovered. After this disaster Hanson removed the remainder of his family to the house of his brother 'who, says Belknap' though of the same religious persuasion yet had a number of lusty sons and always kept his fire-arms in good order for the purpose of shooting game."

Mr. Hanson soon after the attack went to Canada to ransom his family; the following item from the News-Letter of 1725 is of interest in that connection:

"Newport. Aug. 27, (1725) On Tuesday last (Aug. 24) arrived here Mr. John Hanson, Dover, Piscataqua, and about a Month's time from Canade, but last from New York, with his wife & three children and a Servant Woman, as also one Ebenezer Downs, having a wife & five children at Piscataqua, also one Miles Thompson, a Boy, who were all taken Captives about Twelve Months since, by the Enemy Indians, and carried to Canada, except Mr Hanson, who at the same time lost Two of his sons by the Indians; & now it hath cost him about £700 for their Ransom, including his other necessary charges He likewise informs, That another of his children, a Young Woman of about Seventeen Years of Age was carried Captive at the same time with the rest of his Family, with whom he conversed for several Hours, but could not obtain her Ransom, for the Indians would not consent to part with her on any terms, so he was obliged to leave her

Mr Hanson got home 1 Sept 1725, but he could not content himself while his daughter Sarah was in Canada, and about the 19th of April, 1727, started in company with a kinsman who with his wife was bound on a similarly sad errand to redeem children, but he was taken sick on the journey and died about half way between Albany and Canada The daughter married a Frenchman and never returned"

Mr Hodgdon was taxed in Dover in 1741, at which time he was called an Ensign In the several deeds given by him, he is called a housewright, as well as a yeoman He probably followed both vocations

May 15, 1722, Israel sold William Twombly a tract of eight acres of land, situated at Barbadoes (Dover), being part of a grant of sixty acres of land at Salmon Falls, which were granted to Israel Hodgdon, sen

Sept 9, 1741, Israel Hodgdon, jun, sold David Drew twenty acres of land on the westerly side of Bellamy's Bank, above Merritt's Mill.

Apr 28, 1741, Israel Hodgdon, jun, sold Benjamin Allen 76 acres of land at Rochester, being lot No 119

Feb 17, 1753, Israel, with his children, Timothy Caleb, Elijah Estes and Sarah his wife, sold their interest in an estate at Nock's Marsh, which belonged to John Hanson, deceased

Apr 28, 1755, Israel of Dover (at this time the word junior

was left off from his name), for £374, old tenor, sold Joseph Wentworth of Somersworth 25 acres of land, laid out above Great Falls, bounded by the river

Jul 2, 1765, Israel sold his son Peter Hodgdon, certain land at Nottingham, containing 93 acres, adjoining town of Barrington

"Israel Hodgdon of Dover, yeoman, for £500, sells Stephen Evans, my homestead farm, lying at a place called Nock's Marsh in Dover, where I now dwell, containing 120 acres, Beginning at ye Southeasterly corner of Benjamin Evans' land, adjoining on and to ye westerly side of ye road leading from Littleworth, so called, to Bellaman Bank River and running to the River, with all buildings &c"

Dated, Jan 1, 1768

N H records, vol 89, p 479

"Benjamin Page of Weare, for £525, sells Israel Hodgdon of Dover, a certain tract of land in Kensington, being the place on which I lately dwelt, containing 100 acres, bounded Northerly by a road leading from Drinkwater Road over the Red Oak Ridge, Westerly by land of David Green, in part, land of Elisha Prescott, in part, and land belonging to the heirs of Ebenezer Prescott, deceased, in part, Southerly by Stumphill Road, Easterly by land of Elisha Chase, in part, and by land of James Fogg, in part, together with the buildings thereon Also five acres of fresh meadow at Greasy Swamp"

Dated, Feb 9, 1768

N H deeds, vol 89 p 502

Sept 24, 1777, he sold the homestead to his son Caleb for £500, giving a deed of the farm purchased of Benjamin Page, with this addition

"Also another piece of land I purchased of Elisha Prescott, Sept 2, 1772, containing 21 1-2 acres, excepting ten acres which I sold my son Peter Hodgdon"

Dated, Sept 24, 1777

Will dated, May 18, 1779, "Gives daughter Sarah Estes, 5s, gives sons. Timothy, Caleb, Edmund, Israel, Peter, John and Moses, each 5s; to daughter Abigail 5s, gives wife Mary, all my buildings where I now live, with all movable estate" Probated, Apr 25, 1780 Children

355 Sarah Hodgdon,[5] +
356 Timothy Hodgdon,[5] +
357 Caleb Hodgdon,[5] +
358 Edmund Hodgdon,[5] +
359 Israel Hodgdon,[5] +
360 Peter Hodgdon,[5] +
361 John Hodgdon,[5] +
362 Abigail Hodgdon,[5] +
363 Moses Hodgdon,[5] +

MOSES Hodgdon (99), b in Dover, N H, Apr 7, 1702, m in Kittery, Me, July 4, 1723, Sarah, dau of Thomas and Sarah (Furbish) Thompson, b in Kittery, Sept 22, 1702 He and his wife were members of the First Church in South Berwick which was organized 1702 They were dismissed from that church and with others, formed the "Blackberry Hill" church in 1755, he was elected an Elder shortly after the church was organized and held the office until his death Feb 4, 1782, she d in Berwick, Aug 2, 1781 Children

364 Joshua Hodsdon,[5] +
365 Moses Hodsdon,[5] bapt Oct 1, 1727, d young
366 Israel Hodsdon,[5] +
367 Thomas Hodsdon,[5] bapt Nov 8, 1733, d young
368 Sarah Hodsdon,[5] bapt Aug 31, 1735, m ——— Worster
369 Moses Hodsdon,[5] +

SHADRACH Hodgdon[4] (100), b in Dover, N H, about 1709; m 1731-2, Mary, dau. of Joseph and Tamson (Meserve) Ham, b in Dover, Dec 28, 1706 They lived on the homestead which his father deeded him Feb 26, 1731. He was a member of the Fourth Provincial Congress, and was at times called Captain In 1777, he was a member of the General Assembly, when he was styled Major Shadrach, with his wife Mary and two children, were baptized in the First Church, Dover, Oct 10,

1736, and for many years served as deacon He d in Dover, Nov 15, 1791, aged 82 years, she d Mar 19, 1796, aged 90 years Children

370 Ann Hodgdon,[5] bapt Oct 10, 1736
371 Israel Hodgdon,[5] bapt Oct 10, 1736
372 Joseph Hodgdon,[5] bapt Oct 23, 1737
373 Mary Hodgdon,[5] bapt June 15, 1740
374 Shadrach Hodgdon,[5] bapt Feb 4, 1742.
375 Abigail Hodgdon,[5] bapt June 9, 1745
376. Susanna Hodgdon,[5] bapt May 10, 1747
377 Daniel Hodgdon,[5] bapt May 6, 1750

MARY Hodgdon[4] (102), b in Dover, N H, about 1700, m about 1720, Nathaniel, son of Richard and Elizabeth Randall They lived in Durham, N H, where he d Mar 9, 1749, administration on his estate was granted to his widow and the estate was divided Apr. 25, 1759, she d Jan 2, 1775 Children

378 Simon Randall,[5] bapt First Church Dover, May 9, 1725
379 Jonathan Randall,[5] bapt Oct 25, 1730

ABIGAIL Hodsdon[4] (103), b in Berwick, Me, July 16, 1700, m Dec 26, 1721, Bial, son of David and Anna (Jackson) Hamilton, b in what is now Rollinsford, N H, 1676 She was his second wife, he having m (1) Mary, dau of William Heard, they lived in South Berwick His will was written, 1758, probated 1763 Children:

380 Joshua Hamilton,[5] bapt June 7, 1724
381 Jeremiah Hamilton,[5] bapt June, 1725, m June 21, 1758, Sarah Hamilton
382 Joseph Hamilton,[5] +
383 Abigail Hamilton,[5] b about 1729, m Jan 5, 1751, John Turner Bolthood
384 Jonas Hamilton,[5] bapt Apr 5, 1731, m Dec 29, 1757, Charity, dau of John and Charity (Hooper) Key, bapt June 23, 1737

385 Solomon Hamilton,[5] +

386 Susanna Hamilton,[5] bapt June 21, 1739, m. July 13, 1788, Edward Haggens

BENJAMIN Hodsdon[4] (104), b in Berwick, Me, Jan 23, 1702, published, Sept. 8, 1722, with Mary, dau of Samuel and Mary (Rhodes) Shorey, b in Eliot, Me, Sept 23, 1702 They lived in Berwick, where he d in 1774, as shown by will Children:

387 Benjamin Hodsdon,[5] +

388 Stephen Hodsdon,[5] bapt Dec 24, 1727

389 A son,[5] bapt July 7, 1728

390 Mary Hodsdon,[5] bapt July 7, 1728, m. William Frost

391 Elizabeth Hodsdon,[5] bapt. Apr 18, 1731, m Joshua Smith

392 Joseph Hodsdon,[5] bapt Aug 1, 1736

393 Lydia Hodsdon,[5] bapt Aug 1, 1736, m Stephen Hodsdon[4] (146)

394 Jacob Hodsdon,[5] +

395 James Hodsdon,[5] bapt. Mar 27, 1743-4, m Dec 19, 1765, Sarah, dau of Hugh and Hester (Gowen) Ross.

396 Nathan Hodsdon,[5] bapt Dec 10, 1745, m Mar 26, 1772, Mary Barrons

AMY Hodsdon[4] (105), b. in Berwick, Me, Nov 22, 1704, m Mar 15, 1725, Dea John, son of Samuel and Mary (Rhodes) Shorey, b Aug 10, 1704, in Eliot, Me She d and he m (2) Mary, dau of Samuel Clark of Portsmouth, N H, his will was written in 1762 Child

397 Amy Shorey,[5] ——m. Landers Grant, bapt Sept 11, 1726

MARGARET Hodsdon[4] (107), b in Berwick, Me, bapt Apr 19, 1716, with her brother and sisters, b about 1708, m in 1728, Gabriel, son of Gabriel and Mary Hamilton, bapt Sept 6, 1713, with his brother and sisters, b about 1705. They lived in Berwick, where his will was written June 6, 1776, probated Nov 6, 1783. Children

398 Mary Hamilton,[6] +

399 Jerusha Hamilton,[5] bapt July 19, 1730, m about 1751, Thomas Cook of York, Me

400 Gabriel Hamilton,[6] +

401 Amy Hamilton,[5] bapt May 19, 1734, m Dec 18, 1752, Benjamin Kilgore

402 Sarah Hamilton,[5] bapt Nov 16, 1735, m Lord

403. Reuben Hamilton,[5] bapt July 20, 1740, not mentioned in his father's will

404 Simeon Hamilton,[5] bapt June 14, 1741, m Apr 9, 1766, Mary Hearl

405 Silas Hamilton,[5] bapt July 6, 1743, not mentioned in his father's will

406 Margery Hamilton,[5] ——— m ——— Carlisle

407 Lydia Hamilton,[5] +

408 Patience Hamilton,[5] ——— m. ——— Gray

409 Elijah Hamilton,[5] ——— m in 1779, Lydia, dau of Ephraim and Sarah (Walker) Joy, b in Berwick, May 29, 1762

ABIGAIL Hodsdon[4] (112), b in Berwick, Me, Aug 16, 1724, m Nov 25, 1747, Joseph, son of William and Mary (———) Chadbourne, b in Berwick, June 1, 1720 She d and he m (2) Nov 19, 1762, Mrs Mary (Grant) Hamilton, she d and he m (3) Sally Hodsdon, who d July 31, 1803 He d Jan 15, 1808 Children

410 Joseph Chadbourne,[5] bapt June 26, 1748, m Sept 12, 1771, Martha, dau of John and Mary (Grant) Hamilton, bapt Jan 24, 1753 He d at Little Falls, Me

411 Prudence Chadbourne,[5] bapt July 7, 1749, m (1) Andrew Clark, m (2) Enoch Chase

412 Mary Chadbourne,[6] b ———, m Feb 20, 1779 Nathaniel, son of John and Abigail (Goodwin) Guptill, bapt July 24, 1754

413. Scammon Chadbourne,[5] b ———, pub May 8, 1777, with Hannah, dau of Thomas and Mary (———) Guptill, bapt Mar 12, 1747. He was a Revolutionary soldier
414 Mark Chadbourne,[5] b in 1753, m Peggy Beck of Portsmouth, N H, where they lived
415 Benjamin Chadbourne,[5] b ———, m Mary Walker He was a Revolutionary soldier and d in the South
416. Japhet Chadbourne,[5] b ———, was a Revolutionary soldier and was lost at sea
417 Sarah Chadbourne[5] (?)

DANIEL Hodsdon[4] (113), b in Berwick, Me, bapt June 11, 1727, m Aug. 31, 1749, Patience, widow of Daniel Grant They lived in South Berwick Children.

418 Hannah Hodsdon,[5] bapt Dec 6, 1755
419 Samuel Hodsdon,[5] bapt Dec 6, 1755, m Dec 7, 1785, Anna Libby

THOMAS Hodsdon[4] (115), b in Berwick, Me, bapt July 5, 1730, m (1) Sarah, dau of Caleb Seaver of Roxbury, Mass, m (2) Mar 5, 1761, Rebecca, dau of Rev John and Elizabeth (Pratt) Emerson

PRUDENCE Hodsdon[4] (116), b in Berwick, Me, bapt. Sept 24, 1732, m July 18, 1753, Joseph, son of Richard and Mary (Goodwin) Lord, b in Kittery, Me, July 26, 1728, they lived in South Berwick Children

420 Martha Lord,[5] bapt. Feb 21, 1754
421 Jeremiah Lord,[5] bapt. Mar 4, 1754
422 Richard Lord,[5] bapt. Feb 1, 1756, m Mary, dau of Benjamin and Elizabeth (Hill) Gerrish, bapt Jan 2, 1761
423 Joseph Lord,[5] bapt May 20, 1758, d young
424 Eunice Lord,[5] bapt Jan 31, 1762
425 Joseph Lord,[5] bapt July 24, 1764
426 Samuel Lord,[5] bapt Dec 19, 1766

427 Joel Lord,[6] bapt May 8, 1768
428 William Lord,[6] +

RICHARD Hodsdon[4] (119), b in Berwick, Me, ——— m Judith, dau of Phillip and Judith (Heard) Fall, b in Kittery, Me, Apr 3, 1719 They lived in South Berwick and she administered his estate in 1804 Children

429 Margaret Hodsdon,[5] bapt in Berwick, May 15, 1745, m Feb 21, 1771, Jeremiah,[5] son of Thomas and Mary ——— Hodsdon[4] (455)
430 David Hodsdon,[5] bapt Nov 15, 1745, m Sarah ———, will written in 1807
431. William Hodsdon,[5] +
432 Robert Hodsdon,[5] living in Berwick, 1810
433 Andrew Hodsdon,[5] living in Berwick, 1810

SARAH Hodsdon[4] (122), b in Berwick, Me, bapt Oct 26, 1741, m Mar 6, 1753, Stephen, son of Simon and Martha (Lord) Emery, b Mar 21, 1730 He was an Elder in the Free Baptist Church at Kittery, Me Children

434 Stephen Emery,[5] +
435 Joshua Emery,[5] +
436 Jacob Emery,[5] +
437 Simon Emery,[5] +
438 Abigail Emery,[5] b in 1761; m Ebenezer Nowell of York, Me
439. Prudence Emery,[5] +
440 George Emery,[5] +
441 Dominicus Emery,[5] +
442 Mary Emery,[6] b. 1768, d unm
443 William Emery,[5] b in 1770, a physician in New Orleans, La
444 Ichabod Emery,[6] +

JOHN Hodsdon[4] (124), b in Berwick, Me, bapt July 26, 1713, m Elizabeth ———; m (2) pub. Mar 29, 1766, with Abigail Gowen Administration of his estate granted to son Stephen, April 12, 1769 Children.

445. Timothy Hodsdon,[5] bapt Sept 7, 1750
446 James Hodsdon,[5] bapt Sept 7, 1750
447 Daniel Hodsdon,[5] bapt Sept 7, 1750.
448 Stephen Hodsdon,[5] +

THOMAS Hodsdon[4] (124 a), b in Berwick, Me, bapt Mar. 20, 1715, m Mary ——— They lived in South Berwick, will written June 3, 1774-7, probated Jan, 1794. Children

449 Thomas Hodsdon,[5] +
450 Sarah Hodsdon,[5] bapt June 6, 1742, m about 1800, Ebenezer Lord of Lebanon, Me, as his second wife
451 Eunice Hodsdon,[5] bapt Aug 9, 1747; m Oct 18, 1768, Ebenezer Heard
452 Amy Hodsdon,[5] +
453 Mary Hodsdon,[5] bapt in 1740, m ——— Grant
454 Daniel Hodsdon,[5] bapt in 1745, m in Portsmouth, N H, Dec 17, 1777, Sarah Woorster
455 Jeremiah Hodsdon,[5] b ———, m Margaret Hodsdon[5] (429)
456 Benjamin Hodsdon,[5] b ———, m Apr 20, 1780, Sarah Lord, probably dau of Jeremiah and Sarah (Grant-Hamilton) Lord, bapt in South Berwick, July 22, 1761

MARY Hodsdon[4] (125), b in Berwick, Me, bapt Jan 28, 1717; m in 1738-9, William, son of John, Jr, and Grizzel (Grant) Key, b in Berwick, Feb 4, 1703 They lived in South Berwick Children

457 John Key,[5] bapt Feb 17, 1739-40, m Apr 9, 1767, Mehitable Early
458. Ann Key,[5] bapt Jan 10, 1741-2
495 Mary Key,[5] +

460 Hannah Key,[5] +
461 Daniel Key,[5] bapt June 24, 1748

MARY Shackley[4] (127), b in Berwick, Me, Nov 6, 1711, m about 1732, Samuel, son of Samuel and Martha (Wentworth) Lord, b in Kittery, Me, about 1712 They lived in South Berwick, where he d. Feb 7, 1774, date of her death not given Children

462 Mary Lord,[5] +
463 Samuel Lord,[5] +
464 Dorcas Lord,[5] bapt Jan 1, 1738, d Jan 16, 1772
465 Paul Lord,[5] bapt Jan 4, 1742, m Jan 27, 1782, Hannah Frost
466 Isaac Lord,[5] bapt Jan 1, 1744, not named in his father's will.
467 Abigail Lord,[5] bapt Mar 20, 1748, living in 1773
468 Catherine Lord,[5] bapt April 1, 1750, not mentioned in her father's will
469 Margery Lord,[5] named in her father's will, m Sept 15, 1768, Edward Demsey
470 Mark Lord,[5] bapt June 7, 1752, d Mar 23, 1821
471 Martha Lord,[5] bapt Mar 25, 1755, not mentioned in her father's will

RICHARD Shackley, Jr[4] (129), b in Berwick, Me, Mar 8, 1714, m (1) Martha, dau of Daniel and Mary (Lord-Hodsdon) Emery, b in Berwick, June 24, 1721 She d and he m (2) July 12, 1762, Sarah (———), widow of Elijah Goodwin, Sen, of Berwick, who d 1757 Mr Shackley was a deacon in the Congregational Church in South Berwick Children.

472 Daniel Shackley,[5] bapt Nov 23, 1740.
473 Sarah Shackley,[5] bapt Jan 8, 1742, m Apr 27, 1762, Elijah, son of Abraham and Martha (Gowen) Lord, bapt May 17, 1741 They settled in Lebanon, Me
474 Martha Shackley,[5] bapt Nov 15, 1743
475 Hannah Shackley,[5] bapt Sept 6, 1745, d young

476 Richard Shackley, 3d,[5] +

477 Hannah Shackley,[5] bapt Sept, 1748, m May 8, 1770, Elijah Goodwin, Jr

478 Elizabeth Shackley,[5] bapt Apr 21, 1752

479 Lois Shackley,[5] bapt May 1, 1754, d young

480 Mary Shackley,[5] bapt Aug 23, 1759, m Apr 29, 1781, Benjamin, son of Taylor and Elizabeth (Nason) Goodwin, bapt Nov 30, 1754

481 Thomas Shackley,[5] b ——, m. Apr 27, 1775, Bridget Nason

482. Lois Shackley,[5] bapt June 1, 1760, m Apr 29, 1784, Ichabod, son of Nathan and Elizabeth (Shackley) Lord, bapt in Berwick, Apr 2, 1758

MIRIAM Shackley[4] (130), b in Berwick, Me, bapt. Nov 10, 1717, m Patrick[4] (142), son of Nicholas and Abigail (Hodsdon) Gowen, b. in Kittery, Me, Mar 30, 1707 Children

483 Samuel Gowen,[5] a soldier at Fort Ticonderoga in 1758

484 Patrick Gowen, Jr,[5] b ——; m ——, Abigail ——, and lived in Lebanon, Me

ABIGAIL Shackley[4] (131), b in Berwick, Me, bapt Dec 11, 1720, m. Samuel, son of Simon and Margaret (Lord) Emery, b in 1732, pub. Feb 28, 1756

SAMUEL Shackley[4] (132), b in Berwick, Me, bapt July 8, 1722, m May 21, 1745, Amy, dau of Richard and Mary (Goodwin) Lord, b in Kittery, Me, Nov 26, 1724, and settled in Kennebunk, Me Children

485 John Shackley,[5] bapt Oct 11, 1750, m June 1, 1773, Sarah Nason, was then of Wells, Me.

486 Richard Shackley.[5]

487 Joseph Shackley[5]

488. Thomas Shackley[5]

489 Ebenezer Shackley[5]

490 Keziah Shackley.[5]

491 Mary Shackley [5]

JOHN Shackley[4] (133), b in Berwick, Me, bapt Oct 18, 1724, m Nov 13, 1751, Eunice, dau of Benjamin and Mary (Neal) Hill, b in Kittery, Me, Nov 6, 1730 Children

492 Daniel Shackley,[5] bapt May 12, 1754, d young

493 Daniel Shackley,[5] bapt in Eliot, Me, Mar 3, 1756

ELIZABETH Shackley[4] (134), b in Berwick, Me, bapt Jan 16, 1727, m Aug 1, 1751, Nathan, son of Richard and Mary (Goodwin) Lord, b. in Kittery, Me, Dec 5, 1718 They lived in South Berwick Children

494 Nathan Lord, Jr,[5] bapt Sept 5, 1756, m Mar 25, 1784, Elizabeth Haggens

495 Ichabod Lord,[5] bapt Apr 2, 1758, m Lois Shackley[5] (482)

496 Olive Lord,[5] bapt June 30, 1760

497. Elizabeth Lord,[5] bapt Apr 18, 1763, d young

498 Jonathan Lord,[5] bapt Oct 9, 1763, d young

499 Jonathan Lord,[5] bapt June 3, 1765

500 Hannah Lord,[5] bapt July 31, 1767

501 Jotham Lord,[5] bapt Jan 6, 1769, m Nov 9, 1800, Betsey[6], dau of David and Lydia (Stacy[5] [234],) Furbish

502 Elizabeth Lord,[5] bapt Dec 27, 1773

SARAH Shackley[4] (135), b in Berwick, Me, bapt Jan 16, 1727, m June 27, 1751, Daniel, son of Daniel Jr, and Mary (Lord-Hodsdon) Emery, b in Kittery, Me, Aug 18, 1731 They lived in Berwick Children:

503 Sarah Emery,[5] bapt Aug 7, 1757, m Sept 8, 1775, Stephen, son of Stephen and Sarah (Hodsdon) Emery, b in Kittery, Me, Dec 1753

504 Daniel Emery,[5] bapt Mar 25, 1759, m Olive Lord and lived in Eliot

505. Nahum Emery,[5] bapt Oct 30, 1763, m (1) Rhoda Emery,

m (2) Eunice Hodsdon, m. (3) Sarah Pickernell
Rhoda,[6] a dau by second marriage, m William Pike

506 Nathan Emery,[5] bapt Oct 30, 1763, m Hannah Kingsbury

507 Joel Emery,[5] bapt Sept 1, 1765

508 Hosea Emery,[5] bapt May 30, 1767

ABIGAIL Gowen[4] (136), b in Kittery, Me, bapt Apr 12, 1695, m Feb. 14, 1713, Miles, son of Bartholomew Thompson, b Feb 15, 1689 They lived in South Berwick, Me Children:

509 Katharine Thompson,[5] bapt Mar 23, 1727

510 Bartholomew Thompson,[5] +

511 Miles Thompson,[5] bapt Mar 23, 1727; d in 1748

512 Abigail Thompson,[5] bapt Mar 23, 1727, d young

513 Miriam Thompson,[5] +

514 Mary Thompson,[5] bapt Mar 23, 1727

515 Nicholas Thompson,[5] bapt Nov 24, 1728, settled in Falmouth, now Westbrook, Me

516 Amy Thompson,[5] bapt Sept 1, 1734

517 Elizabeth Thompson,[5] bapt June 20, 1736

518 Abigail Thompson,[5] bapt Mar 22, 1740, d young

519 Abigail Thompson,[5] bapt Oct 3, 1742

ELIZABETH Gowen[4] (137), b in Kittery, Me, bapt July 5, 1697, m Dec 8, 1718, Joseph Hart, b in Lynn, Mass, Sept 12, 1689 They lived in Berwick, Me, where he d, 1769 Children:

520 Ruth Hart,[5] +

521 Moses Hart,[5] b in Berwick, bapt Dec 4, 1720

522 Elias Hart,[5] bapt Feb 3, 1722

523 Elizabeth Hart,[5] } bapt Nov 29, 1724

524 Abigail Hart,[5] } bapt Nov 29, 1724

525 Joseph Hart,[5] bapt Mar 23, 1727

526 A child,[5] bapt Oct 13, 1728

527 John Hart,[5] bapt May 2, 1731

MARGARET Gowen[4] (138), b in Kittery, Me, Mar 19,

1699, m Apr 10, 1717, Abraham, son of Nathan, Jr, and Martha (Tozier) Lord, b in Kittery, Oct 29, 1699 They lived in Kittery His will was dated Apr 11, 1772, probated Apr 20, 1779 She d Feb. 11, 1775 Children

528 Simeon Lord,[5] bapt Oct 11, 1719
529 Benjamin Meads Lord,[5] +
530 Abraham Lord,[5] +
531 Nathan Lord,[5] bapt Dec 1, 1723, m Elizabeth Shackley[4] (134)
532 Nicholas Lord,[5] +
533 Joshua Lord,[5] bapt May 5, 1728
534 Jeremiah Lord,[5] +
535 David Lord,[5] +
536 Solomon Lord,[5] bapt June 2, 1734
537 Elijah Lord,[5] bapt May 17, 1741, m Apr 27, 1762, Sarah Shackley[5] (473), and settled in Lebanon, Me
538. Margaret Lord,[5] +
539 Sarah Lord,[5] b in Kittery, m July 29, 1762, Samuel, son of Thomas and Abigail (———) Jellison, b in South Berwick, Me, bapt Aug 5, 1739

HESTER Gowen[4] (139), b in Kittery, Me, Nov 20, 1701, m Feb 19, 1727, Hugh Ross, who came from Belfast, Ireland, and lived in the northern part of Eliot, Me Hester d and he m (2) Patience ———, by whom he had eight children. According to Tate's Journal Hugh Ross of Berwick, Me, was buried Mar 2, 1776 Children

540 William Ross,[5] bapt June, 1732, m Mrs Sarah (Chadbourne) Smith
541 John Ross,[5] bapt Oct 6, 1734
542 Sarah Ross,[5] b ———, m Dec 19, 1765, James, son of James and Mary (Shorey) Hodsdon, bapt Mar 27, 1744

WILLIAM Gowen[4] (141), b in Kittery, Me, Apr. 4, 1705, m June 24, 1724, his cousin Jane, dau. of John and Mercy (Hammond) Gowen, b in Kittery, May 13, 1706 William was a scout in John Wheelwright's company in 1722, d in 1748 Mrs Gowen d in Boston, Mass, Sept 20, 1750 Children

543 William Gowen,[5] +
544 Nicholas Gowen,[5] b May 4, 1729, pub Oct 5, 1751, with Keziah Cole of Wells, Me
545 George Gowen,[5] b May 15, 1733, m 1755, Abigail Martin
546 Mary Gowen,[5] b Aug 1, 1736, m Oct 6, 1750, Elijah Kingsbury of York, Me
547 John Gowen,[5] +
548 Jane Gowen,[5] b Mar 20, 1743

ANNA Gowen[4] (143), b in Kittery, Me, June 29, 1709; m Dec 9, 1724, Richard, son of Jonathan and Mary (———) Thurlo of Newbury, Mass, where they had a family of children

Hon JAMES Gowen[4] (144), b in Kittery, Me, Feb 14, 1715; m (1) Nov 29, 1738, Anna, dau of William and Sarah (Gowen) Smith, she d and he m (2) before 1769, Lois, dau of John and Elizabeth (Norton) Woodbridge, b Apr 28, 1725 He was a captain, selectman twenty years, Judge of the Court of Common Pleas seven years, representative to General Court seven years, and Governor's Council 1770-4 He was a cornet in the Blue Troop of Horse in 1757, and captain in Jedediah Preble's regiment at Fort Ticonderoga in 1758. He d about 1781, his widow, Lois, d about 1813 Judge Gowen lived in the part of Kittery, now Eliot, Me, where his house, built in 1730, was known as "The Shapleigh House," being occupied by his youngest daughter and her family It was standing until Apr, 1899, a little north of the schoolhouse in district number one Children

549 Sarah Gowen,[5] +
550 Abigail Gowen,[5] +
551 Elizabeth Gowen,[5] +
552 Phebe Gowen,[5] +
553 Anna Gowen,[5] +

HOMESTEAD OF HON. JAMES GOWEN

554 Mary Gowen,[6] +
555 Louise Gowen,[6] +

JOHN Hodsdon[4] (145), b in Berwick, Me, bapt Aug 29, 1736, m Martha ———, and he seems to have d young, as his widow and children are said to have been in the Bermuda or Bahama Islands Children

556 John Hodsdon,[5] with his mother in the Bermudas or Bahama Islands
557 Martha Hodsdon,[5] in the Bermudas or Bahama Islands

STEPHEN Hodsdon[6] (146), b in Berwick, Me, bapt with his brother, Aug 29, 1736 m (1) Lydia, dau of Benjamin and Mary (Shorey) Hodsdon, bapt in Berwick, Aug 1, 1736, she d Nov 6, 1774, and he m (2) Sept 21, 1775, Elizabeth, dau of Capt John and Elizabeth (Malcolm) Wise, bapt Dec 11, 1743 Child

557 a John Hodsdon,[5] +

JUDITH Horn[4] (147), b in Dover, N H, Aug 16, 1721, she was a member of the First Church, Dover, m Henry Buzzell and lived in Dover Children

558 Nathaniel Buzzell,[5] bapt in Dover, July 31, 1740
559 Jane Buzzell,[5] bapt in Dover, Aug 25, 1743

JAMES Ferguson[4] (156), b in Kittery, Me, about 1700, m in 1727, Patience, dau of Joshua and Sarah (Hatch) Downing, b Feb. 9, 1710 They lived on the old homestead now Eliot Me, where he d Widow Patience administered his estate in 1766; she d in 1789 Children ·

560 James Ferguson,[5] b in Eliot, m Apr 24, 1749, Elizabeth Stanley b Jan 29, 1724
561 Daniel Ferguson,[5] +
562 Robert Ferguson,[5]
563 Elizabeth Ferguson,[6] +
564 Dennis Ferguson,[5] +

565 Stephen Ferguson,[5] +
566 William Ferguson,[5] +
567 Sarah Ferguson,[5] b Mar 16, 1739, m as his (2) wife Sept 28, 1775, Joseph, son of Joseph and Elizabeth (Meads) Furbish
568 Reuben Ferguson,[5] +

SARAH Morrell[4] (157), b in Eliot, Me, Dec 1, 1695, m June 14, 1716, Benjamin, son of Benjamin and Mary ——— Weymouth, b in Dover, N H, Feb 1, 1694 He received a grant of land from his father in 1724 Jan 21, 1721, they were both baptized and united with the First Church in South Berwick, Me Children

569 Benjamin Weymouth,[5] bapt Jan 21, 1721-2
570 Mary Weymouth,[5] bapt Jan 21, 1721-2
571 Abigail Weymouth,[5] bapt Aug 4, 1723
572 Elizabeth Weymouth,[5] bapt May 21, 1727

JOHN Morrell[4] (159), b in Eliot, Me, July 6, 1701, m June 16, 1721, Mary, dau of Thomas and Tamsen (Gowell) Hanscom, b in Kittery, Me, July 28, 1700 They settled in Scarborough, Me Children

573 Martha Morrell,[5]
574 Eleanor Morrell,[5]

ROBERT Morrell[4] (160), b in Eliot, Me, Feb 18, 1704, m May 29, 1729, Sarah Roberts of Dover, N H, who d Aug 14, 1737, m (2) in 1738, Patience Weymouth[4] (54 b), she d and he m (3) Nov 9, 1779, Anna Jones Will written 1781, probated 1784 Children

575 Abigail Morrell,[5] b in Eliot, Jan 28, 1731, m Apr 15, 1750, Thomas Hammett of Newington, N H.
576 Lucy Morrell,[5] b Nov 2, 1732
577 William Morrell,[5] b Mar 5, 1734, m Mar 1, 1764, Rachel, dau of Gilbert and Abigail (———) War-

ren, bapt July 8, 1736

578 Lydia Morrell,[5] b Dec, 1735

579 Isaac Morrell,[5] b Jan 31, 1739, m May 28, 1772, Joanna, dau of William and Phebe (———) Chadbourne, she d and he m (2) July 4, 1793, Hannah Stanley

580 Nicholas Morrell,[5] +

581 Timothy Morrell,[5] b July 16, 1742

582 Joel Morrell,[5] +

583 Mary Morrell,[5] b Nov 12, 1746, m in Dover, N H, Dec 21, 1778, Silas Hoag of Newtown

584 Anne Morrell,[5] b May 16, 1749, m ——— Hunt

585 Eunice Morrell,[5] b Oct 24, 1751

586 Jane Morrell,[5] b Oct 9, 1758, m Dec 13, 1781, Joseph Broughton of Portsmouth, N H

JOHN Morrell[4] (162), b in Kittery, Me, July 30, 1702, m Dec 16, 1722, Ruth Dow of Hampton, N H, his will was written 1780, probated in 1784, it names only the first three children, the rest perhaps d young Children

587. Miriam Morrell,[5] b May 25, 1728, m Aug 24, 1744, Ebenezer Hussey

588. Hannah Morrell,[5] b Apr 26, 1731, m Dec 1, 1748, Gideon Warren

589 Peace Morrell,[5] b Mar 16, 1733, m Moses Purington

590 Keziah Morrell,[5] b Sept 30, 1735

591 Pelatiah Morrell,[5] b May 8, 1741

592 Mary Morrell,[5] b Mar 1, 1744

593 Susanna Morrell[5]

594 William Pepperrell Morrell[5]

PETER Morrell[4] (164), b in Kittery, Me, Sept 16, 1709, m Oct 10, 1731, Sarah Peaslee of Hampton, N H They lived in North Berwick, Me, she d June 19, 1780, he m (2) Elizabeth Sawyer, he d Nov 11, 1801 Children

595 Thomas Morrell,[5] +

596 John Morrell,[5] +

597 Sarah Morrell,[5] b Mar 23, 1736, killed by Indians in North Berwick, May 9, 1748
598 Stephen Morrell,[5] +
599 Jacob Morrell,[5] +
600 David Morrell,[5] +
601 Jonathan Morrell,[5] b July 9, 1742, d June 15, 1743
502 Ruth Morrell,[5] +
603 Peaslee Morrell,[5] +
604 Peter Morrell,[5] +

JEDEDIAH Morrell[4] (165), b in Kittery, Me, Aug 29, 1711, m (1) Dec 5, 1734, Elizabeth, dau of Reynold and Elizabeth (Tancy) Jenkins, she d and he m (2) Oct 20, 1737, Anna Dow, who d May 21, 1761 He m (3) Jan 28, 1862, Sarah Gould He belonged to the Society of Friends in North Berwick, Me, he was a farmer, lumberman, blacksmith, trader and physician He d in 1776. Children:

605 Abraham Morrell,[5] b Aug 23, 1735, d young
606 Abraham Morrell,[5] b Dec 26, 1738; m (1) Elizabeth Lewis, m (2) Sarah Nichols
607 Josiah Morrell,[5] b ———, m Oct 25, 1764, Hannah Webber, he d in Litchfield, Me
608 Winthrop Morrell,[5] b Dec 20, 1744, m Susannah Lewis
609 John Morrell,[5] b ———, m (1) Sarah Varney, m (2) Elizabeth G Baker
610 Peace Morrell,[5] named in her father's will, m Daniel Perkins of Wells, Me., in 1783

MARY Morrell[4] (168), b. in Kittery, Me, m as his second wife, 1738, William, son of Capt Nathaniel and Bridget (Vaughn) Gerrish, bapt July 16, 1710 Capt William Gerrish d in Berwick, Me, Aug 8, 1794-5, aged 90 Children

611 Joseph Gerrish,[5] b. Feb 19, d Mar 29, 1738
612 Bridget Gerrish,[5] +
613 Hannah Gerrish,[5] bapt Mar 4, 1742, d young
614. Jedediah Gerrish,[5] bapt. Jan 13, 1745, d young

615 Hannah Gerrish,[5] +
616 Margaret Gerrish,[5] bapt July 9, 1750, m Phineas Frost
617 Nathaniel Gerrish,[5] bapt July 1, 1753; d young
618 John Gerrish,[5] bapt Aug 29, 1756, m Feb 14, 1778, Mary Hardison
619 Mary Gerrish,[5] +
620 Martha Gerrish,[5] +
621 Elizabeth Gerrish,[5] +

RICHARD Nason[4] (169), b in Kittery, Me Feb 14, 1703, m Nov 5, 1725, Abigail, dau of David and Eleanor (———) Libby, b in Kittery, Sept. 29, 1707 This family moved to Cape Elizabeth, Me Children:

622 Ephraim Nason,[5] +
623 Eleanor Nason,[5] +
624 Abigail Nason,[5] +
625 Sarah Nason,[5] +
626 Richard Nason,[5] +
627 Isaac Nason,[5] +
628 Jonathan Nason,[5] +
629 Uriah Nason,[5] +
630 Adah Nason,[5] +
631 Elizabeth Nason,[5] +

JOHN Nason[4] (170), b in Kittery, Me Oct. 24, 1704, m. pub Aug 31, 1734, with Margaret Lord His will was dated Mar 2, 1744, probated Apr 4, 1748; he probably d a soldier at Cape Breton Children.

632 Margaret Nason,[5] +
633 John Nason,[5] bapt Mar 15, 1739
634 Eunice Nason,[5] +
635 Uriah Nason,[5] +

MARY Nason[4] (171), b in Kittery, Me, Nov 30, 1706, m Sept, 3, 1730, Mathew, son of Mathew and Elizabeth (Brown)

Libby, b in Kittery He was a farmer in Eliot, Me, d in 1760 Children

636 Jerusha Libby,[5] b Mar 3, 1731, m Nov 30, 1762, Benjamin Staples
637 Mathew Libby,[5] +
638 Zebulon Libby,[5] +
639 Azariah Libby,[5] +
640 William Libby,[5] +

SARAH Nason[4] (172), b in Kittery, Me, Nov 25, 1708, m Dec 25, 1729, James, son of James and Margaret (Goodwin) Frost, b in Berwick, Me, Nov 5, 1707 They lived in South Berwick, where their children were baptized Children

641 Joseph Frost,[5] bapt Sept 3, 1732, d young
642 James Frost,[5] bapt Sept 3, 1732, d young
643 Sarah Frost,[5] bapt Jan 23, 1735, d young
644 Sarah Frost,[5] bapt May 30, 1736
645 Joseph Frost,[5] bapt June 18, 1738
646 Mary Frost,[5] bapt June 15, 1740
647 James Frost,[5] bapt Sept 9, 1744
648 Simon Frost,[5] bapt Sept 22, 1747
649 Jeremiah Frost,[5] bapt Apr 9, 1749
650 Jerusha Frost,[5] bapt Nov 10, 1752
651 Tinny Frost,[5] bapt June 24, 1756

URIAH Nason[4] (174), b in Kittery, Me, Jan 31, 1713, pub Nov 1, 1740, with Sarah Stone, in Wells, Me, he d in 1742, his widow, Sarah, m Dec 2, 1743, James Boston, in Wells Child

652 Jeremiah Nason,[5] b Sept 23, 1741

ADAH Nason[4] (175), b in Kittery, Me, Jan 6, 1715, m Dec 3, 1747, Benjamin Wormwood of Wells, Me, she d aged 99

AZARIAH Nason[4] (176), b in Kittery, or Berwick, Me, July 25, 1716, m pub Mar 27, 1742, with Abigail, dau of James and Mary (Tetherly) Staples, b. in Kittery, Aug. 21, 1720. He d. in 1787. Children:

653. James Nason,[5] +
654. Reuben Nason,[5] d. in the Revolutionary Army, Sept. 30, 1776.
655. Azariah Nason,[5] +
656. John Nason,[5] +
657. Adah Nason,[5] m. Jan. 5, 1775, Joseph Norton.
658. Elizabeth Nason,[5] m. Aug. 20, 1778, Pelatiah Wittum.
659. Stephen Nason,[5] +
660. Nathaniel Nason,[5] +
661. Mary Nason,[5] m. in Portsmouth, N. H., Jan. 16, 1772, John Hickey.

PHILADELPHIA Nason[4] (177), b. in Berwick, Me., Dec. 28, 1719; m. (1) Jan. 12, 1742, James Rankin of Wells, Me.; he d. and she m. (2) Aug. 12, 1756, John Harvey; she d. aged 102 years.

ELIZABETH Nason[4] (179), b. in Berwick, Me., May 27, 1727; m. Feb. 7, 1750, James Goold; she d. and he m. (2) Hannah, dau. of Rev. John Harvey, and lived in Arundale, Me. He was a soldier in Sir William Pepperrell's regiment in 1757, and was in the expedition to Canada that year. He d. in Biddeford, Me., in 1810. Widow Hannah m. in 1812, Col. Caleb Emery. James Goold had twenty children and we are not sure how many were Elizabeth Nason's. Children:

662. Elizabeth Goold.[5]
663. Mary Goold.[5]
664. Joseph Goold.[5]
665. Hannah Goold.[5]
666. John Goold.[5]
667. Benjamin Goold.[5]
668. Lyman Gould.[5]
669. Alexander Goold.[5]

ADAH Tidy[4] (181), b. in Kittery, Me., Jan. 22, 1716; m. Nov.

4, 1735, Joshua, son of Daniel and Margaret (Gowen) Emery, b in Kittery, June 30, 1715 Through his influence the first Baptist Church was organized in Berwick, Me, June 28, 1768, in which he was an elder and preacher He d Feb, 1797, she d. in 1815 Children

670 Margaret Emery,[5] b Oct 20, 1739, m Jan 24, 1777, David Blaisdell of York, Me

671 Adah Emery,[5] b June 29, 1741; m John Emery.

672 Meribah Emery,[5] bapt Aug 20, 1754

673 Hannah Emery,[5] b in 1756, m Oct 7, 1771, Jedediah, son of James and Margaret (Wallingford) Goodwin, bapt in Berwick, May 18, 1746.

ELIZABETH Drowne[4] (186), b in Boston, Mass, Apr 20, 1700, m Mar 12, 1721, in Kittery, Me, James Wittum, probably son of Peter and second wife, Eunice

SAMUEL Drowne[4] (187), b. in Boston, Mass, July 5, 1704, m ———, his children were baptized in Dover, N H, in 1736 Children

674 Elizabeth Drowne,[5] bapt in Dover, May 29, 1736

675 Samuel Drowne,[5] bapt in Dover, May 29, 1736

MERCY Vickers[4] (191), b in Hull, Mass, Sept 14, 1711, m Dec 5, 1732, Peter Porter, and lived in Hingham, Mass Child

676 Elizabeth Porter,[5] b in Hingham, Sept. 9, 1733, m Andrew Burrell of Weymouth, Mass

GEORGE Vickers[4] (192), b in Hull, Mass, Nov 12, 1713; m May 1, 1735, Lydia, dau of Hezekiah and Elizabeth (Whitten) Tower, b in Hingham, Mass, May 1, 1717 Child

677 Sylvanus Vickers,[5] b Apr 10, d Apr 25, 1736

ELIZABETH Lewis[4] (195), b in Hingham, Mass, July 19, 1719, m Sept 30, 1739, David, son of David and Rebecca (Stodder) Beal, b in Hingham, July 24, 1712 They lived in Hingham, where she d Mar 9, 1766; he d June 4, 1799. Children

678 Joseph Beal,[5] +
679 Jacob Beal,[5] +
680 James Beal,[5] +
681 Elizabeth Beal,[5] b June 5, 1746, d Oct 11, 1827
682 Mary Beal,[5] b May 22, 1748, d Sept 27, 1752
683 Rebecca Beal,[5] b Apr 5, 1750, d Jan, 1823
684 A Child,[5] b and d Aug 27, 1752
685 David Beal,[5] b Feb 17, 1755, d Dec 22, 1829

GEORGE Lewis,[4] (196), b in Hingham, Mass, July 23, 1721, m. ———, Susanna Hall He was a tailor in West Hingham, where she d. May 14, 1790, he d Sept 27, 1795 Children.

686 Olive Lewis,[5] +
687. David Dixon Lewis[5], b Mar 24, 1748, d Aug 25, 1751
688 Caty Lewis,[5] +
689 Abigail Lewis,[5] b Feb 20, d Mar 28, 1752
690 A child,[5] b and d May 3, 1754

SAMUEL Lewis[4] (199), b in Hingham. Mass, Oct 28, 1725, m July 16, 1750, Sarah, dau of John and Sarah (Hobart) Humphery, b in Hingham, Mar 19, 1730, he d May 26, 1786 Children

691 Joseph Lewis,[5] b July 19, 1752
692. Sarah Lewis,[5] b Oct 22, 1753
693 Josiah Lewis,[5] b Jan 26, 1755
694 Deborah Lewis,[5] +

EBENEZER Lewis[4] (201), b in Hingham, Mass, July 21, 1728, m Nov 14, 1751, Hannah, dau of Jeremiah and Elizabeth (Gilbert) Hersey, b in Hingham, Mar 8, 1729, d June 25, 1790, he d Nov 19, 1803 Children:

695 Mehitable Lewis,[5] +
696 Abigail Lewis,[5] +

697 Ebenezer Lewis,[5] +
698. William Lewis [5]
699 Ebed Lewis,[5] b Dec 3, 1759
700 Hannah Lewis,[5] b June 12, 1767

HANNAH Lewis[4] (203), b in Hingham, Mass, Dec 3, 1731; d Jan 21, 1789 The will of Hannah Lewis "Single woman", dated Jan 18, 1789, proved Mar 31, 1788, gives to Abigail, wife of Zadock Hersey, "my riding hood and my cambleteen gown, to my cousin Eliza Beal my bengal gown, to my cousin Rebecca Beal my round calico gown, to my cousin Hannah Lewis my Irish camblet gown, to Susanna Beal, dau of Elijah my old calico and to Catherine Beal her sister my silk and worsted gown All the residue of my estate I give to my sister Lucy Lewis"

LYDIA Vickers[4] (205), b in Hingham, Mass, bapt Nov 11, 1722, m (1) Dec 30, 1745, Ambrose, 3rd, son of Ambrose and Sarah (Beal) Lowe, b in Hingham, Dec 30, 1720, he d Feb 4, 1750, she m (2) Dec 17, 1758, Joshua Gould, he d and she m (3) July 6, 1775, as his second wife, Jeremiah Stodder, b in Hingham, Nov 2, 1709 He was a shipwright in Hingham, where he d July 2, 1790, she d June 1, 1800 Children

701 Israel Lowe,[6] b Dec 24, 1746.
702 Lydia Lowe,[6] b Oct 7, 1748, m Oct. 12, 1777, as his second wife, Elijah, son of David and Sarah (Beal) Loring, b in Hingham, Aug 20, 1745
703 Joshua Gould,[5] b June 29, 1759

CALEB HODGDON[5] (357), b in Dover, N H, Jan 27, 1732-3; m (1) in Dover, about 1756, Priscilla, dau of Nathaniel and Catherine (Neal) Austin, b in Dover, May 4, 1732 They lived in Dover, where she d Feb 21, 1773 He m (2) Elizabeth, dau. of William Twombly of Dover, bapt Sept 21, 1740 He was in the Revolutionary war We find in the printed records of "New Hampshire in the Revolution," p 235, "A return of Capt Caleb Hodgdon's Company on Seavey's Island, Nov 5, 1775,

HOMESTEAD OF MAJ. CALEB HODGDON

Caleb Hodgdon Capt " Page 253, "Return of the troops in New Hampshire Dec 6, 1775, Capt Caleb Hodgdon's Company Page 367, "Field and Staff officers of Col Pierce Long's regiment Major Caleb Hodgdon, Dover"

July 18, 1774, he was chosen one of a committee of five, to meet at Exeter, and appoint Delegates to join in a General Congress of the Colonies He was chosen representative from Dover for the years, 1774, '77, '78 and 82 June 15, 1778, he was appointed a committe to hire men for service in Rhode Island In 1785, he was chosen as 2nd Lieut Colonel of the regiment of Artillery of Dover June 24, 1786, he was nominated a Special Justice of the Superior Court for Strafford County, to act in certain cases

William Twombly of Dover, Gentleman, for £300, sells Caleb Hodgdon of Dover, Mariner, 60 acres or the whole of my homestead farm in Dover
Dated, Jan 23, 177–.
(Strafford County deeds, vol I, p 12)

"Caleb Hodgdon of Dover for £300, sells his son Hanson Hodgdon of Kensington, A certain parcel of land in Kensington, whereon the said Hanson now lives, containing 107 acres, also 5 acres of meadow ground in Greasy Swamp, so called, which pieces of land is the same and all the same that I purchased of my late father Israel Hodgdon of said Kensington, as by his deed"
Dated, Sept 9, 1791
(Strafford County deeds, vol 129, p 536)

Maj Caleb lived on the Hodgdon farm at Dover, situated on the banks of Back River, not far from "Sawyer's Mills" It is occupied by the descendants of his youngest son, William Hodgdon In early life he seems to have been a mariner engaged in the West India trade, but after the Revolution devoted himself to farming and looking after large tracts of lumber land, which were granted him in Carroll County

His will was written Feb 17, 1810, probated May 28, 1811, from which we give the following extracts —"Gives wife Elizabeth, use of his house &c 2 cows, horse and sheep and part of the homestead farm

Gives son Hanson Hodgdon, one dollar with what he had before

Gives daughter Hannah Clark, wife of William Clark, one half of the dwelling house and lot of land where they now live

Gives daughter Sarah Footman, wife of Jonathan G Footman, one half of the house and lot of land where they now live

Gives son Joshua Hodgdon, all the land in Ossipee, where the said Joshua now lives

Gives son Israel Hodgdon, 120 acres of land in Wakefield, and other property there

Gives daughter Priscilla Watson, wife of Samuel Watson, $400 and other property

Gives granddaughter, Caroline Hodgdon $60 and other property

Gives son William Hodgdon, the homestead farm &c and the rest of my estate not otherwise disposed of, William to be the executor

Witnessed by Peggy Gage, A Baker, Daniel Hanson and William Twombly "

Strafford County Probate Records

Maj Hodgdon d in Dover, Apr 30, 1814, his widow, Elizabeth, Sept 1, 1829 Children:

704 Hanson Hodgdon,[6] +
705 Hannah Hodgdon,[6] +
706 Nathaniel Hodgdon,[6] b in Dover, June 1, 1761, not mentioned in his father's will
707 Elijah Hodgdon,[6] b in Dover, Apr 4, 1765, not mentioned in his father's will
708 Caleb Hodgdon, Jr,[6] +
709 Joshua Hodgdon,[6] +
710 Israel Hodgdon,[6] +
711 Moses Hodgdon,[6] b in Dover, Feb 14, 1773, his mother died the 21st, and he is not mentioned in his father's will
712 Sarah Hodgdon,[6] +
713 Priscilla Hodgdon,[6] +
714 William Hodgdon,[6] +

ISRAEL HODGDON
Taken in 1861, aged 90

HANSON Hodgdon[6] (704), b. in Dover, N. H., Jan. 4, 1758, m. in Dover, Feb. 19, 1784, Mary, dau. of Capt. Alexander Caldwell, bapt. in Dover, Aug. 23, 1769, the record states that she was bapt. in private, and was ten years of age.

HANNAH Hodgdon[6] (705), b. in Dover, N. H., Sept. 9, 1759, m. Oct. 13, 1792, William Hanson Clarke, b. Nov. 12, 1767. They were members of the First Church of Dover, where she d. Apr. 12, 1843, he d. in Dover, Feb. 19, 1844. We have not found record of children.

CALEB Hodgdon[6] (708), b. in Dover, N. H., 1767, m. May 21, 1798, Mrs. Lucy (Dennett) Mann, widow of Peter Mann of Dover. Caleb lived in Dover, where he d. Nov. 6, 1800. Child:

715. Caroline Hodgdon,[7] +

JOSHUA Hodgdon[6] (709), b. in Dover, N. H., Feb. 3, 1769, m. Sept. 20, 1792, Martha Libby, b. in Dover, Mar. 22, 1771. They lived in Dover and Ossipee, N. H., where he was a farmer on "Pocket Mountain", he d. in Ossipee, Aug. 29, 1855. His widow d. in Newburyport, Mass., Nov. 27, 1858. Children:

716. Lydia Hodgdon,[7] b. in Dover, Apr. 20, d. May 18, 1793.
717. Elijah Hodgdon,[7] +
718. Caleb Hodgdon,[7] +
719. Lydia Hodgdon,[7] +
720. James Hodgdon,[7] +
721. Charles Hodgdon,[7] b. July 13, 1804, d. in Ossipee, May 7, 1813.
722. Martha Hodgdon,[7] +
723. Hannah Hodgdon,[7] +
724. Adriel Hodgdon,[7] +
725. Charles Hodgdon,[7] +

ISRAEL Hodgdon[6] (710), b. in Dover, N. H., Apr. 29, 1771, m. in 1793, Margaret Clark, b. Oct. 28, 1770. He was a farmer in Dover, Wakefield and Milan, N H He was the first of the family to settle in the wilds of Milan Taking a willow staff in his hand, he walked from Ossipee, and when he reached "Hodgdon Hill" (Milan), he put it in the ground, where it took root, and is now a flourishing tree, in whose shadow his large family might gather She d in Milan, Sept 12, 1849, he d. there Feb 20, 1862 Children:

726 Elizabeth Hodgdon,[7] +
727 Lucy Hodgdon,[7] b Sept 29, 1796, d young
728 Moses Hodgdon,[7] b Mar 22, 1799, d young
729 Moses Hodgdon[7] +
730 Hanson Hodgdon,[7] +
731 William Clark Hodgdon,[7] +
732 John Hodgdon,[7] +
733 Jane Hodgdon,[7] +

SARAH Hodgdon[6] (712), b in Dover, N H; m July 9, 1805, Jonathan Gage, son of Thomas and Susannah (Gage) Footman, b in Dover, Dec 29, 1782, he d at sea

PRISCILLA Hodgdon[6] (713), b in Dover, N H, Jan 31, 1779, m Sept 19, 1803, Samuel, son of Benjamin and Lydia (Hanson) Watson, b in Dover, July 7, 1774, she d Oct 1, 1822, he d Apr 14, 1847 Children.

734 Nancy Watson,[7] +
735 Elizabeth Watson[7]
736 Horace P Watson,[7] +
737 Susan Watson,[7] b Oct 2, 1810, d Mar 10, 1811
738 Lydia Watson[7]
739 Lucy Watson,[7] b Dec 21, 1815, d Sept 2, 1817

WILLIAM Hodgdon[6] (714), b in Dover, N H, Aug 13, 1774; m Jan 30, 1817, Susan, dau of Eliphalet and Patience (Evans) Coffin, b in Dover, Mar 26, 1778, they lived on the homestead, and he was executor of his father's will She d Mar 24, 1842, he d Jan 16, 1842 Child:

740 Elizabeth Hodgdon,[7] +

CAROLINE Hodgdon[7] (715), b in Dover, N H, in 1800, m in Dover, Oct 13, 1825, Charles Baker of Portland, Maine

ELIJAH Hodgdon[7] (717), b in Dover, N H, July 17, 1794, moved with his parents to Ossipee, when a child, he m Sally, dau of James Clark and ——— (Smith) Scates He d in Ossipee, June 21, 1869

CALEB Hodgdon[7] (718), b in Ossipee, N H, Apr 30, 1796, m (1) Sarah Roberts, m (2) Mary Champion, m (3) Clarissa Preble He d in Ossipee, July 3, 1868 Children

741 Joel Hodgdon[8]
742 Freeman Hodgdon,[8] m Altheda Pray
743 Sarah Hodgdon,[8] m Frank Severs
744 Hannah Hodgdon,[8] m ——— Pike
745 Martha Hodgdon,[8] m ——— Goldsmith

LYDIA Hodgdon[7] (719), b in Ossipee, N H, Dec 26, 1800, m in Ossipee, in 1820, Amasa Fogg, b July 12, 1797, he was a farmer in Ossipee and Milan, N H He d Oct 16, 1872, she d Nov 23, 1892 Children

746 Mary J Fogg,[8] b in Ossipee, June 3, 1821, living in Milan
747 Martha H Fogg,[8] b in Milan, Dec. 13, 1822, d May 7, 1833
748 Athalinda M Fogg,[8] b in Milan, Jan 18, 1826, d July 12, 1847
749 Nathan Fogg,[8] +
750 Sarah Fogg,[8] +
751 Elijah Fogg,[8] b in Milan, Aug 18, 1833, d in Milan, Oct 22, 1898
752 Martha H Fogg,[8] +
753 Lydia Fogg,[8] b April 9, 1839, d Oct 16, 1840
754. Lydia H. Fogg,[8] +

755 Emeline Burbank Fogg,[8] +

JAMES Hodgdon[7] (720), b in Ossipee, N H., Oct 1, 1802, m ——— Peavey of Barnstead, N H, they lived in Newburyport, Mass, he d Jan 14, 1870 Children:

756 William Hodgdon,[8] b, d
757. Cyrus Hodgdon,[8] b
758 Angie Hodgdon,[8] b, m ——— Wheeler
759 Emily Hodgdon,[8] b, m

MARTHA Hodgdon[7] (722), b in Ossipee, N H, Apr 11, 1806, m Milton Smart of Newburyport, Mass, where she d Aug 29, 1875 Child

760 Harrison Smart,[8] +

HANNAH Hodgdon[7] (723), b in Ossipee, N H, Feb 16, 1810, m June 1, 1832, Ira Edwin, son of John and Hannah (Batchelder) Sanborn, b in Parsonsfield, Me, Mar 4, 1806 He was a broker in Boston, Mass, where he d Jan 14, 1859, she d Aug 14, 1870, in Boston Children

761 Ira Edwin Sanborn,[8] +
762 Charles Henry Sanborn,[8] +
763 John Murry Sanborn,[8] +
764 Washington Irving Sanborn,[8] +
765. Hannah Hodgdon Sanborn,[8] b Dec 1, 1838, d 1841.
766 Martha Ann Sanborn,[8] b Aug 30, 1840, d Sept 22, 1893
767 Hannah Hodgdon Sanborn,[8] b May 29, 1843; d Aug 20, 1892
768 Lydia Ellen Sanborn,[8] b and d 1846

ADRIEL Huzzey Hodgdon[7] (724), b in Ossipee, N H, July 11, 1812; m in Salisbury, Mass, Mary Swett, dau of Daniel and Annie (Swett) Fowler, b in Salisbury, May 7, 1812 They lived in Ossipee until 1844, then in Newburyport, Ipswich and Wen-

MOSES HODGDON

MRS. MOSES HODGDON

ham, Mass, where he d Dec 11, 1902, she is living in Newbury-port, with her daughter Children

769 Ruth Ann Hodgdon,[8] +
770 Leander Fowler Hodgdon,[8] +

CHARLES Hodgdon[7] (725), b in Ossipee, N H, Nov 25, 1817, m Oct 18, 1839, Naomi, dau of John and Polly (Wentworth) Roberts, b in Wakefield, N H, June 19, 1816 They lived in Newburyport, Mass, and later returned to Ossipee, where he d May 1, 1886, she d July 20, 1890 Children

771 Charles Henry Hodgdon,[8] +
772 John Hodgdon,[8] +
773 Albert Joshua Hodgdon,[8] +
774. Susan Ellen Hodgdon,[8] b May 7, 1851, d Oct 15, 1854
775 Mary Susan Hodgdon,[8] + }
776 Sarah Ellen Hodgdon,[8] + }

ELIZABETH Hodgdon[7] (726), b in Dover, N H, Apr 6, 1794, m Aug 4, 1814, Joseph Dam, Jr, of Dover Children

776a Harriet Dam.[8]
776b Calvin Dam[8]
776c Lorenzo Dam[8]
776d Samuel Dam[8]
776e Sarah Dam[8]

MOSES Hodgdon[7] (759), b in Dover, N H, Oct 22, 1800, m Mrs Sally (Mathers) Fogg, dau of John and Catherine (Tuttle) Mathers, b Dec 13, 1796 She m (1) 1815, Daniel Fogg of Ossipee, N H, who d in 1820 By this marriage she had one dau, Sally, b in Ossipee, Jan 28, 1817, who m Nov, 1837, Simon F Cole of West Milan, N H Mr Cole was for many years well known among business men in that section, also in Portland, Me, where he d Feb 21, 1882 After his death Mrs Cole spent most of her time with her children in Minneapolis, Minn and

Berlin, N H, making the journey between the East and West many times Mrs Cole was a very interesting woman and delighted in telling the young people of the privations of those early days, as she moved with her father Mr Hodgdon when eleven years of age into the woods in Milan there being only one framed house in the town (1828) nothing but log huts, with roofs of bark, held down with rocks They used to lie in bed and hear the wolves howl, there was little chance for schooling, sometimes the school was kept in the barn, sometimes in the "front-room" of one of the houses, Sally learned to write on birch-bark, and never had a pencil unless she made it herself Mrs Cole had seven children four of whom are living, she also had fourteen grand and twenty great grand children Although eighty-seven years of age she made the journey from Minneapolis to Berlin this present summer (1904) unattended She d in Berlin, Aug 9, 1904 Mr. Hodgdon was a farmer in Ossipee, having moved there with his father when young, where he remained until 1828, when he settled in Milan and they bore with others the burdens and privations of the early settler Mrs Hodgdon d in Milan, Jan, 1869, he d Sept, 1881 Children.

777. Lucy Jane Hodgdon,[8] b Aug 31, 1821, d young
778. Samuel Fox Hodgdon,[8] +
779 Moses Hodgdon, Jr,[8] +
780 Elizabeth F. Hodgdon,[8] +
781 Daniel F Hodgdon,[8] b Apr 5, 1830, d young
782 Charles Norman Hodgdon,[8] +
783 Daniel F Hodgdon,[8] b Sept 5, 1837, d Sept 1, 1860
784 Emily Hodgdon,[8] +
785 Ruth A Hodgdon,[8] +

HANSON Hodgdon[7] (730), b in Dover, N H, Jan 30, 1803, m about 1822, Abbie, dau of James Clark and ——— (Smith) Scates, b in Ossipee, N H, Sept 27, 1801 They lived in Ossipee, Milan, Jackson and Farmington, N H, where he d Oct 2, 1873, Mrs Hodgdon d in Livermore, Me., Apr 7, 1892 Children

HANSON HODGDON

WILLIAM C. HODGDON

786 Anna Maria Hodgdon,[8] b in Ossipee, June, 1823, d in Jackson, 1835

787 Israel Warren Hodgdon,[8] b in Milan, Feb 11, 1826, d in Farmington, Sept , 1848

788 Frances Dianah Hodgdon,[8] +

789 James Clark Scates Hodgdon,[8] +

790 Ruth Anna Hodgdon,[8] b in Jackson, N H , Apr 6, 1835 , d in Farmington, Apr , 1841

791 Andrew Jackson Hodgdon,[8] +

792 Hanson Hodgdon,[8] b in Farmington, Mar 8, d Apr , 1839

793. David Taylor Parker Hodgdon,[8] +

794 Sarah Lizzie Hodgdon,[8] b in Farmington, Apr 4, 1843 , d. in Hartford, Me , Jan 2, 1865

WILLIAM C Hodgdon[7] (731), b. in Dover, N H , Oct 5, 1806; m in Freedom, N H , Dec 28, 1826, Olive Dearborn Perkins, b in Biddeford, Me , Dec 14, 1801 They lived in Ossipee and Stark, N H , where he was justice of the peace for many years Mr Hodgdon was commissioned Ensign of the 8th Company of Infantry in the 24th Regiment of Militia in the state of New Hampshire by Gov William Badger, Sept 22, 1834 , also commissioned Lieutenant in the same Company, Mar 1, 1836 Apr 3, 1839, Lieut. Hodgdon was honorably discharged at his own request These papers are in the possession of his daughter, Miss Olive Hodgdon of Methuen, Mass Mr Hodgdon later moved to Biddeford, where he d Feb 16, 1882 , she d in Biddeford, Apr 13, 1889 Children

795 William Clark Hodgdon, Jr ,[8] +

796. Rebecca Perkins Hodgdon,[8] +

797. A daughter,[8] } b Mar 28 . d Apr 8, 1835
798. A daughter,[8] }

799 Maria Harmon Hodgdon,[8] b in Stark, Mar 14, 1836 , d in Biddeford, Apr 10, 1847

800 Olive Dearborn Hodgdon,[8] b in Stark, Dec 9, 1838 , living in Methuen, Mass

801 Mary Hodgdon,[8] b in Stark, June 18, 1841, d in Biddeford, July 1, 1844

JOHN Hodgdon[7] (732), b in Wakefield, N H, Mar 28, 1809, m Dec 27, 1830, Fannie C Hagar, b Mar 21, 1814, in Milan, N H He was a farmer in northern New Hampshire until 1857, when they removed to the West, settling in Sharon, Wis, where he was active in the planning of the town and erected all of the first buildings The first post-office was established in 1858, with Mr Hodgdon as postmaster, he held the office until 1861, when he again took up his trade as architect, which he followed until a few years before his death He d in Sharon, June 15, 1886, Mrs Hodgdon d in Janesville, Wis, Feb 21, 1899 Children:

802 Harriet D Hodgdon,[8] +
803 Lucy F Hodgdon,[8] b in Somersworth, N H, Sept 20, 1834, d Aug 11, 1835
804. George W Hodgdon,[8] +
805 Joseph W Hodgdon,[8] +
806 Caroline W. Hodgdon,[8] +
807 Fordice C B Hodgdon,[8] +
808 Helen M Hodgdon,[8] +
809 Flora E Hodgdon,[8] +

JANE Hodgdon[7] (733), b in Wakefield, N H, Nov 24, 1811; she moved when a child with her parents to Milan, N H She m Joseph Demeritt, b July 1, 1813, he d. June 20, 1857, she d. Oct 9, 1881 Children:

810 Mary Elizabeth Demeritt,[8] +
811 Sarah Ann Demeritt,[8] +
812 Matilda Jane Demeritt,[8] +

NANCY Watson[7] (734), b. in Dover, N H, Feb 1, 1804, m Mar 20, 1824, Stephen Davis of Dover She d Jan 24, 1849 Child:

JOHN HODGDON

813 Ann Elizabeth Davis[8]

HORACE P Watson[7] (736), b in Dover, N H, about 1808, m Betsey C Ham of Rochester, N H

ELIZABETH Hodgdon[7] (740), b in Dover, N H, Oct 15, 1819, m (1) Oct 5, 1837, James W, son of James and Harriet (Fiske) Cowan, b in Pleasant Valley, N Y, June 23, 1814 He was a practicing physician in Dover, where he d July 22, 1848, she m (2) Nov 12, 1857, William Howe of Dover, he d Oct 14, 1887, she d Jan 18, 1888 Children:

814 Susan Ellen Cowan,[8] +
815 William H Cowan,[8] b Feb 27, 1842, d June 16, 1852
816 James Fiske Cowan,[8] b July 9, 1844, d Oct 27, 1850

NATHAN Fogg[8] (749), b in Milan, N H, Sept 13, 1828, living on the homestead in West Milan with a large family, but we could not get the records

SARAH Fogg[8] (750), b in Milan, N. H, Aug 3, 1831, m ——— Buswell and lived in East Kingston, N H, where she d Feb 10, 1902

MARTHA H Fogg[8] (752), b in Milan, N H, Aug 27, 1836, m ——— Sias and lived in Ossipee, N H, where she d Oct 1, 1869

EMELINE B Fogg[8] (755), b in Milan, N H, May 11, 1845, m in Ossipee, N H, in 1866, Albert Stillings of Ossipee They settled in Rochester, N H, where they now reside Children

817 Ernest Fogg Stillings,[9] b June 6, 1876
818 Mary Ellen Stillings,[9] +

HARRISON Smart[8] (760), b in Newburyport, Mass, ———, m Martha Cole and lived in Newburyport Children

819 George Smart,[9] m Annie Ross and live in Newburyport.

820 Mary Abbie Smart,[9] m Wendell Plummer and live in Ohio

821 Milton Smart,[9] m Mary DeFord

IRA E Sanborn[8] (761), b in Parsonsfield, Me., Apr 27, 1833; m Sept 4, 1860, Marilla Susan Nash of Addison, Me, b Feb 24, 1835 Mr Sanborn was a salesman in Boston, Mass, where she d Jan 18, 1891, he d Dec 31, 1893 Children

822 Lizzie Maira Sanborn,[9] +

823 Frank Edwin Sanborn,[9] +

CHARLES H Sanborn[8] (762), b in Parsonsfield, Me, June 10, 1834, m Dec 30, 1861, Mrs Maria A (O'Leary) Nugent He served as captain in the 28th Massachusetts Infantry in the Civil War, he d Dec 15, 1867

JOHN M Sanborn[8] (763), b in Parsonsfield, Me, Jan 16, 1836, m Nov, 1858, Abigail W C Slade. Mr Sanborn was editor of a paper in Boston, Mass, where he d May 8, 1861, she m (2) John Shaw Child

824 John Walter Sanborn,[9] +

Maj WASHINGTON I Sanborn[8] (764), b in Parsonsfield, Me, Dec 24, 1836, he was appointed second Lieut of the Washington Territory Infantry, Oct, 1862, Aide-de-Camp to General Benjamin Alvord, commanding the Department of Colorado, June 23, 1864, Captain and Assistant Adjutant General of Volunteers, Feb 1, 1865, 1st Lieut 13th United States Infantry, May 11, 1866, Capt, Dec, 1884 He m Nov 1, 1866, Clara W Hawkes, now retired as Major and living in Los Angeles, Cal, a member of Loyal Legion and Sons of the American Revolution Children

825. Clara Ella Sanborn,[9] +

826 Grace Irving Sanborn,[9] +

RUTH A Hodgdon[8] (769), b in Ossipee, N H, Aug 9,

1834, m in Newburyport, Mass, Aug 10, 1850, Samuel Bliss, son of Solomon and Cynthia (Bliss) Butterfield, b in Haverhill, N H, Jan 22, 1825 They lived in Newburyport, where he d July 13, 1903 Children

827 Isabel Maria Butterfield,[9] +
828 Ruth Anna Butterfield,[9] +
829 George Everett Butterfield,[9] +
830 Willard Ellsworth Butterfield,[9] +
831 Milton Smart Butterfield,[9] +
832 Arthur Lincoln Grant Butterfield,[9] b Nov 29, 1869
833 Florence Isabel Butterfield,[9] (adopted) b Sept 28, 1878

LEANDER F Hodgdon[8] (770), b in Ossipee, N H, May 9, 1837, m Hattie A Brown, b in Lynn, Mass, Oct 14, 1841 He is a carpenter in Lynn, where they reside Children

833 a Charles E Hodgdon,[9] +
834 Leander O Hodgdon,[9] +
835 Benjamin L Hodgdon,[9] +
836 Mary H Hodgdon,[9] b in Lynn, Nov 27, 1866, d May 13, 1868
837 Henry W Hodgdon,[9] +
838 Hattie L Hodgdon,[9] +
839 George E Hodgdon,[9] b Sept 25, 1875, d Aug 30, 1877
840 Martha A Hodgdon,[9] +
841 George G Hodgdon,[9] b in Lynn, Sept 4, 1884

CHARLES H Hodgdon[8] (771), b in Newburyport, Mass, Jan 20, 1840, m Aug 26, 1862, Helen Borontho, dau of Benjamin F and Mary Haven (Whitten) Garland, b in Wolfboro, N H, Mar 12, 1838 They lived in Wolfboro, now Nashua, N H, where he is in the Sash and Blind business Children

842 Adelle Hodgdon,[9] +
843 Mary Josephine Hodgdon,[9] b in Wolfboro, July 19, 1870, graduated from Bates College, Lewiston, Me,

1893, later studied at Chicago University and received her A M degree, and has since been a teacher in the Nashua High School

JOHN Hodgdon[8] (772), b in Newburyport, Mass, June 20, 1817, m Sept 12, 1870, Lucinda Abbott, he was a blacksmith in Haverhill, Mass, for several years, now lives on the homestead in Ossipee, N H

ALBERT J Hodgdon[8] (773), b in Newburyport, Mass, July 29, 1849, m Nov 29, 1877, Mary Adelaide Higgins of Vermont, they live in Ossipee, N H

MARY S Hodgdon[8] (775), b in Ossipee, N H, May 28, 1856, m Nov 23, 1881, George L Young, b in Ossipee, May 11, 1859 They reside in Gonic, Rochester, N H Children

844 Myrtle Young,[9] b in Ossipee, Feb 24, 1883, student at Bates College

845 Elvena Young,[9] b in Ossipee, May 16, 1885; student at Bates College, Lewiston, Me

846 Gladys Young,[9] b in Rochester, May 3, 1894, d young

SARAH E Hodgdon[8] (776), b in Ossipee, N H, May 28, 1856, m Dec 24, 1885, William Penn, son of Thomas and Clarissa (Payne) Higgins, b in Eastham, Mass, Sept 1, 1860 They live in Haverhill, Mass. Children

847 Charles Thomas Higgins,[9] b in Haverhill, Sept 2, 1887, in Haverhill High School, Class of 1906

848 Robert Henry Higgins,[9] b July 20, 1890

849 Edith May Higgins,[9] b Nov 17, 1894

850 Frank Higgins,[9] b Feb 26, 1898

SAMUEL F Hodgdon[8] (778), b in Ossipee, N H, July 13, 1823, m (1) July, 1846, Athelinda Fogg, he is a farmer in Milan, where she d July 10, 1847 He m. (2) Dec 26, 1847, Marie Leavitt, b in Stark, N H, Jan 10, 1830, d June 10,

MR. AND MRS. MOSES HODGDON, JR.

HOMESTEAD OF MOSES HODGDON, JR.

1875, and he m (3) Nov 25, 1876, Abbie Scales, b in Wakefield, N H, Dec 9, 1860 They reside in West Milan Children

851 John Mathers Hodgdon,[9] +
852 Ozmon M Hodgdon,[9] +
853 Iola A Hodgdon,[9] +
854 Daniel Webster Hodgdon,[9] +
855 Ernest Augustus Hodgdon,[9] +
856 Octavia Matilda Hodgdon,[9] b Sept, 1877, m Leslie Hagar[9] (914)
857 Marie C Hodgdon,[9] b Feb 16, 1879, she is training for a nurse in Concord, N H
858 Jerome O Hodgdon,[9] b Oct 5, 1882
859 Georgiana M. Hodgdon,[9] b Feb 10, 1884
860 James O Hodgdon,[9] b Jan 23, 1886
861 Nina Hodgdon,[9] b Feb 23, 1889
862 Samuel Fox Hodgdon, Jr,[9] b Mar 12, 1891
863 Abbie Hodgdon,[9] b Mar 11, 1893
864 Sally Hodgdon,[9] b Nov 11, 1895
865 Ruth Hodgdon,[9] b Apr 27, 1897
866 Hobson Dewey Hodgdon,[9] b. Jan 30, 1899
867 William C Hodgdon,[9] b Dec 4, 1899

MOSES Hodgdon, Jr[8] (779), b in Ossipee, N H, Oct 22, 1825, when four years of age his parents moved to Stark, and one year later to Milan, N H He m in 1853, Lucinda Angeline, dau of Daniel and Polly (Wheeler) Green, b in Berlin, N H, Dec 6, 1834, they lived in West Milan, where she d Sept 4, 1873, he m (2) in 1880, Arvilla Twitchell

He was identified in town and state affairs, having served in the legislature in 1867 and 69 as representative of Milan He also served that town as selectman for fourteen years and tax collector several years He was a lumberman, also contractor and builder, having constructed several buildings in Milan and Berlin, N H, where he settled in 1885, and also served that town both as selectman and assessor

He d at the home of his daughter in Portland, Me, while on a visit to his children in that city, Apr 25, 1903, and was buried in the family cemetery in West Milan Children

868 Melvin Elmer Hodgdon,[9] +
869 Marilla Hodgdon,[9] +
870 Charles Dexter Hodgdon,[9] b Nov 11, 1856, d May 17, 1863
871 Daniel Glenroy Hodgdon,[9] b in West Milan, May 27 1858, he was a mechanic and killed on a rollway at Island Park, Vt, Aug. 10, 1882
872 John Alfred Hodgdon,[9] +
873 Helen Georgiana Hodgdon,[9] +
874 Minnie Estelle Hodgdon,[9] +
875 Walter F Hodgdon,[9] +
876 Moses Alberto Hodgdon,[9] +
877 Charles Dexter Hodgdon,[9] +
878 Lewis Clark Hodgdon,[9] +

ELIZABETH F Hodgdon[8] (780), b in Milan, N H, Jan 30, 1828, m Dexter Wheeler, she d Oct, 1867 Child

879 A daughter,[9] b d

CHARLES N Hodgdon[8] (782), b in Milan, N H, Dec 7, 1833, m Jan, 1862, Elizabeth A Andrews, b Mar. 25, 1841 He was a teacher, farmer and lumberman in Milan until about 1885, when he settled in Berlin, N H, where he engaged in the wood coal and real estate business He is also one of the Directors and Stock-holders of the First National Bank of Berlin, where they reside Children

880 Wilfred Alphonso Hodgdon,[9] +
881 Flora Emily Hodgdon,[9] +
882 Henry Norman Hodgdon,[9] +
883 Mabel Elizabeth Hodgdon,[9] b June 9, 1880

EMILY Hodgdon[8] (784), b in Milan, N H, June 6, 1840, m (1) Dec, 1861, Welcome A Crafts, m (2) Sept 25, 1870,

CHARLES N. HODGDON

JAMES C. S. HODGDON

John H Chandler, proprietor of the Chandler House in Dummer, N. H., where they reside

RUTH A Hodgdon[8] (785), b in Milan, N H, July 6, 1842, m Nov 10, 1864, Lorenzo P Adley They lived in Dummer, N H, where he was killed on the railroad The family resides in Dummer Children

884 James A G Adley,[9] +
885 Ellen E Adley,[9] b Aug 14, 1873

FRANCES D Hodgdon[8] (788), b in Milan, N H, Nov 4, 1829; m in Farmington, N H, in 1849, Rev Edward M Haggett, b in Hartford, Me, July 20, 1827 They lived in Livermore, Me, where he d Jan 1, 1882, she d in Livermore, Oct 29, 1897

JAMES C S Hodgdon[8] (789), b in Milan, N. H, May 9, 1833, m in Lee, Mass., Feb 1, 1859, Mary Elizabeth, dau of Azariah Winchell and Mehitable (Eaton) Brooks, b in Sudbury, Mass, Mar 28, 1837 They lived for a time in St Louis, Mo, where he was manager for George W Wentworth, wholesale dealer in boots and shoes; they removed from there to Davenport, Iowa, where he was a dealer in merchandise He was with the Union Army in 1863-4, at Vicksburg, Miss, connected with the Sutler's department He later settled in Haverhill, Mass, and was engaged in shoe business, then removed to Kansas and took up a ranch, remained a few years and returned to Haverhill Mr Hodgdon was killed in a railroad accident on the Boston and Maine Railroad in Wells, Me, Jan, 2, 1882, when on his way to Livermore, Me, to attend the funeral of his brother-in-law, Rev. Mr Haggett The family resides in Haverhill Children

886 Fred Milton Hodgdon,[9] +
887 Edward James Hodgdon,[9] +
888 Mildred Brooks Hodgdon,[9] b Nov 8, 1874

ANDREW J Hodgdon[8] (791), b in Farmington, N H, Aug

1, 1837; he left home at the age of fifteen and learned the shoemaker's trade in Natick, Mass.; later spent a few years teaching school in Maine and New Hampshire. He enlisted as private in Company C 23rd Regiment of Maine Infantry, Sept. 10, 1862. Mustered into United States service, Sept. 29, 1862, for 9 months. Mustered out and honorably discharged, July, 1863, at Portland, Me., by reason of expiration of term of service. Re-enlisted in Company C 32nd Regiment of Maine Infantry, Feb. 16, 1864, and mustered into the United States service as 1st Sergeant at Augusta, Me., Mar. 11, 1864, for three years. Mustered out and honorably discharged from the service of United States, Dec. 12, 1864, by reason of the consolidation of the 32nd with the 31st Maine Regiment. After his return he was a dealer in Merchandise in Livermore, Me., where he remained but a short time, then settled in Haverhill, Mass., as a shoe contractor and later a manufacturer. Mr. Hodgdon m. in Bethel, Me., Nov. 6, 1869, Olive Emogene, dau. of John and Eliza (Eastman) Carr, b. in Weld, Me., Feb. 14, 1838; he is a dealer in Groceries and Provisions in Haverhill, where she d. Aug. 18, 1901. Mr. Hodgdon is very much interested in the ancestry and genealogy of his family, and it is to this fact we are indebted for this present volume, which he has published with great care and expense. Child:

889. Frances Martha Hodgdon,[9] +

DAVID T. P. Hodgdon[8] (793), b. in Farmington, N. H., Feb. 21, 1841; he was a teacher and merchant in Livermore, Me., where he m. Apr. 26, 1863, Melissa Gardner, dau. of Theodore and Lucy Gardner (Bragg) Russell, b. in Rumford, Me., Oct. 11, 1842. He moved to Haverhill, Mass., where he was a shoe contractor and dealer in sole leather for some years; then settled in Kansas, where he is a ranchman, also editor and proprietor of the Rice County Eagle; they reside in Lyons, Kans. Children:

890. Ida Mabel Hodgdon,[9] +
891. Edith Maude Hodgdon,[9] +

WILLIAM C. Hodgdon, Jr.[8] (795), b. in Ossipee, N. H., Sept.

DAVID T. P. HODGDON

30, 1827, m in Biddeford, Me, Mar 22, 1852, Nancy D Thompson, b in Porter, Me, May 22, 1830 They lived in Holyoke, Mass, now (1904) in Tiverton, R I, where he is a farmer Child

891a Emma Adelia Hodgdon,[9] b in Holyoke, June 26, 1853, d Jan 14, 1854

REBECCA P Hodgdon[8] (796), b in Stark, N H, June 4, 1833, m in Biddeford, Me, Aug 8, 1852, Horace E, son of William and Hannah (Perkins) Wood, b July 4, 1832, in Biddeford, where they lived for a time, then in Fall River, Mass, where he was overseer and superintendent in a cotton mill, now retired, living in Methuen, Mass Child

891b George William Wood,[9] +

HARRIET D Hodgdon[8] (802), b in Milan, N H Dec 20, 1831, m Mar 7, 1853, Levi N Low of Stratford, N H They lived in Sharon, Wis and Brainerd, Minn, where he d June 10, 1899, she d in Duluth, Minn, Mar 19, 1901 Children

892 Leslie Low,[9] +
893 Belle Low,[9] +
894 Fred Eugene Low,[9] +

GEORGE W Hodgdon[8] (804), b in South Berwick, Me, Sept 28, 1836, m in Sharon, Wis, Feb 15, 1860, Jane Helen Dougall of Sharon He d Dec 12, 1880, Mrs Hodgdon lives in Spokane, Wash Children

895 Alvah Melvin Hodgdon,[9] b Nov 3, 1860, d Jan 12, 1862
896 Frank Ellsworth Hodgdon,[9] +
897 Alvah Warren Hodgdon,[9] b July 6, 1863, d July 9, 1873
898 Harriet Ann Hodgdon,[9] +
899 May Hodgdon,[9] + }
900 Maude Hodgdon,[9] + }
901 William Dougall Hodgdon,[9] b Nov 23, 1870
902. Finis Ratchel Hodgdon,[9] b Dec 21, 1872, d Nov 10, 1876

903 George Alexander Hodgdon,[9] +
904 Olive Ratchel Hodgdon,[9] +

JOSEPH W Hodgdon (805), b in Dummer, N H, Dec 20, 1840, m June 22, 1866, Ella Loucks They lived in Janesville, Wis, where he d Sept 11, 1898 Children:

905 Harry H Hodgdon,[9] +
906 Bertha F Hodgdon,[9] +
907 Beulah A Hodgdon,[9] +

CAROLINE W Hodgdon[8] (806), b in Stark, N H, Oct 13, 1843, m Sept 11, 1865, in Sharon, Wis, Jacob Sarasy. They live in Janesville, Wis. Children

908 Eva Sarasy,[9] +
908 a Lottie Sarasy,[9] b Feb 14, 1868, d in infancy
909 Ralph J Sarasy,[9] b in Chicago, Ill, Feb 21, 1871, living in Janesville

FORDICE C B Hodgdon[8] (807), b in Dummer, N H, Oct 9, 1846; moved with his parents to Sharon Wis, in 1857, where he remained for a few years, then went into Iowa, while the country was new and wild He followed railroading, went through Nebraska on the "Union Pacific" in 1867-8, he was once shot with an arrow by an Indian, while on top of a telegraph pole, the arrow pinning his ankle to the pole. He also engaged in mining, as well as becoming a telegraph operator, and now has charge of the Naval Telegraphic Station in Key West, Fla, where he m Dec 9, 1886, Charlotte A Heermans, they reside at Key West

HELEN M Hodgdon[8] (808), b in Dummer, N H, Nov 30, 1849, m in Sharon, Wis. Sept 29, 1874, Robert D Stewart. They reside in Beloit, Wis Children:

910 Ray Stewart,[9] b in Janesville, Wis, Sept 11, 1879
911 Fannie Stewart,[9] +

FORDICE C. B. HODGDON

FLORA E Hodgdon[8] (809), b in Stark, N H, Jan 3, 1856, m in Sharon, Wis, Nov 20, 1875, James Alden, son of James Whipple and Sarah (Adams) Field, b in Sugar Creek, Wis, in 1847 He is a hardware dealer of the firm of Field & Wolcott, Sharon, where they reside Mr Field was a soldier in the Civil War, serving ninety days Children

912 Guy Alden Field,[9] b in Sharon, May 21, 1882, student in the State University at Madison, Wis
913 Forrest Whipple Field,[9] b in Sharon, Sept 16, 1885, student in the State University at Madison

MARY E Demeritt[8] (810), b in Milan, N H, Oct 13, 1836, m Dec 11, 1853, Joel Hagar, b June 2, 1824 They lived in Milan where he d Jan 18, 1888 Child

914 Leslie Hagar,[9] (adopted) +

SARAH A Demeritt[8] (811), b in Milan, N H, May 3, 1838, m in 1855, Andrew J Lang, b July 6, 1837 They lived in Milan where she d Aug 6, 1865, he d Feb 11, 1893 Children

915 William Alphra Lang,[9] b Apr 1, 1856, d Sept 13, 1861
916 Joseph Lang,[9] b in 1858, d young
917 Matilda Lang,[9] b in 1860
918 William Joseph Lang,[9] b Feb 8, d Aug 29, 1863

MATILDA J Demeritt[8] (812), b in Milan, N H, Dec 21, 1841, m Mar 1, 1862, Nelson N Nichols, b Jan 10, 1836 They reside in West Milan Children

919 Mary Elizabeth Nichols,[9] +
920. Charles Henry Nichols,[9] +

SUSAN E Cowan[8] (814), b in Dover, N H, Aug 13, 1839, m Feb 8, 1865, Charles Henry, son of Jonathan and Martha (Perkins) Sawyer, b in Watertown, N Y, Mar 30, 1840 He was a woolen manufacturer in Dover, where she d Apr 20, 1899 Mr Sawyer, now retired, lives on the old Hodgdon homestead in

Dover Children.

920a William Davis Sawyer,[9] +
920b Charles Francis Sawyer,[9] +
920c James Cowan Sawyer,[9] +
920d Edward Sawyer,[9] +
920e Elizabeth Coffin Sawyer,[9] b Mar 8, 1880, living in Dover

MARY E Stillings[9] (818), b in Rochester, N H, Dec 10, 1879, m Dec 9, 1903, Justin A Emery, they reside in Rochester

LIZZIE M Sanborn[9] (822), b in Boston, Mass, June 14, 1861, m Sept 30, 1891, Charles Danforth Nelson, b in Ohio, Aug 13, 1866, graduated at Harvard Medical School, Cambridge, Mass, 1891 He was a practicing physician in Norwalk, Ohio, where they lived Dr Nelson d in Pomona, Cal, Nov 28, 1900, his family now (1904) resides in New Dorchester, Mass Children.

921. Ira Sanborn Nelson,[10] b Dec 29, 1894
922 Aro Danforth Nelson,[10] b Aug 27, 1898

FRANK E Sanborn[9] (823), b in Boston, Mass, Aug 25, 1866, he is a mechanical engineer, was an instructor in Tufts College, now (1904) Director of the Industrial Arts Department in the Ohio State University, Columbus, Ohio He m Jan 1, 1901, Elizabeth Champney Hunneman of Roxbury, Mass, b Mar 21, 1873, they reside in Columbus.

JOHN W Sanborn[9] (824), b in Boston, Mass, Aug 28, 1860, m June 29, 1887, Alice Dean Spear of Quincy, Mass, b Oct 28, 1863 He was head of the large and successful house of J W Sanborn & Co, dealers in optical instruments, and president of the N E Association of Opticians, president of the N E Optical Institute and commodore of the Quincy Yacht Club He d in Quincy, June 11, 1901, Mrs Sanborn resides in Quincy

CLARA E Sanborn[9] (825), b Nov 1, 1867, m June 10, 1891, William P Brayton of Missoula, Mont They reside in Dawson City, Alaska Children

923 Sanborn Pitman Brayton[10]
924 Julius Brayton[10]

GRACE I Sanborn[9] (826), b July 7, 1869, m Oct 6, 1889, Lieut Thomas H McGuire of the 25th United States Infantry He d. and she and her children are living with her father in Los Angeles, Cal Children

925 Irving Sanborn McGuire[10]
926 Katharine McGuire[10]

ISABEL M Butterfield[9] (827), b in Newburyport, Mass, Jan 14, 1851, m June, 1869, Benjamin Goodwin, son of Thomas and ——— (Johnson) Hodgkins, b in Newburyport, Feb. 1843 They lived in Newburyport, Chelsea and Amesbury, Mass, and again in Newburyport, where he d, and she m (2) George T Perkins of Newburyport They reside in Somerville, Mass Children :

927 Fred Albert Ernest Hodgkins,[10] +
928 Alice Maud Blanche Hodgkins,[10] +
929 Mabel Averick Hodgkins,[10] b Aug 18, d Sept, 1874
930 Nettie Ruth May Hodgkins,[10] +
931 Wilbert G Hodgkins,[10] +
932 Edith Isabel Perkins,[10] b Apr 22, 1887, d young.
933 Harold W Perkins,[10] b Nov 3, 1889, d young
934 Helen Isabel Perkins,[10] (adopted) b Nov 12, 1894

RUTH A Butterfield[9] (828), b in Newburyport, Mass, Oct 26, 1854, m in Wenham, Mass, John Pickering Dodge of Wenham, where they lived for a time, now in Beverly, Mass Children

935 Hattie Athalia Dodge,[10] m George Cole
936 Mabel Dodge,[10] m Joseph Perkins
937. George Willard Milton Dodge,[10] +

938 Ruth Ada Dodge,[10] b in 1889

GEORGE E Butterfield[9] (829), b in Newburyport, Mass, Mar 10, 1859, m Rosie Morse They live in Wakefield, Mass, where he keeps a fish market

WILLARD E Butterfield[9] (830), b in Newburyport, Mass, Sept 20, 1862 m Hattie Maria Ordway of Newburyport, where they reside

MILTON S Butterfield[9] (831), b in Newburyport, Mass, Apr 28, 1866, m Fannie Morton Clark, b May 29, 1869 They lived in Newburyport, where she d Sept 19, 1890, he d in Newburyport, Apr 21, 1899 Children

939 Orrie Weston Butterfield,[10] b June 27, 1887
940 Lillian May Butterfield,[10] b Sept 13, 1890

CHARLES E Hodgdon[9] (833), b in Lynn, Mass, Apr 18, 1862, m in Lynn, Sept 14, 1897, Isabelle E Haney, b in Fort Fairfield, Me, Dec 12, 1864 They reside in Lynn, where he is a real estate agent Child.

941 Arthur E Hodgdon,[10] b in Lynn, June 5, 1903

LEANDER O Hodgdon[9] (834), b in Lynn, Mass, Sept 4, 1863, m in Charlestown, Mass, Mar 10, 1889, Anita Maud Morse, b in Bridgetown, Nova Scotia, Sept 5, 1866 They reside in New Bedford, Mass Children.

942 Arthur O Hodgdon,[10] b in New Bedford, Apr 10, d Apr 12, 1891
943 Clarence M Hodgdon,[10] b in New Bedford, Aug 2, 1896

BENJAMIN L Hodgdon[9] (835), b in Lynn, Mass, Mar 9, 1865, m (1) in Lynn, Aug 27, 1887, Jeanette V Harwood, b in 1865 They lived in Lynn, where she d Mar 20, 1888, and he m (2) Oct 21, 1899, Maud S Bossom, they reside in Hopedale, Mass

HENRY W Hodgdon[9] (837), b in Lynn, Mass, Nov 18, 1868, m in Lynn, Sept 2, 1891, May S Wood, b in Lynn, Mar 5, 1869 They reside in Lynn Children

944 Rolland H Hodgdon,[10] b in Lynn, July 31, 1893
945 Donald H Hodgdon,[10] } b June 9, 1897
946 Dorris M Hodgdon,[10] }

HATTIE L Hodgdon[9] (838), b in Lynn, Mass, Oct 15, 1873, m in Lynn, Feb 11, 1892, James H Turnbull, b in Scotland, Feb 14, 1869 They reside in Lynn Child

947 James W Turnbull,[10] b in Lynn, Dec 5, 1892

MARTHA A Hodgdon[9] (840), b in Lynn, Mass, Apr 20, 1879, m in Lynn, Oct 2, 1897, Samuel S Alley, b June 9, 1877 They reside in Wenham, Mass Children

948 Herman R Alley,[10] b in Wenham, Aug 27, 1898
949 Raymond T Alley,[10] b in Wenham, Aug 16, 1900

ADELLE Hodgdon (842), b in Wolfboro, N H, Aug 10, 1865, she was for some years head teacher in the Massachusetts State School for the Feeble Minded at Waverly, Mass She m in Nashua, N H, Aug 4, 1904, Thomas Benjamin, son of Theodore S and Laura F (Overlock) Brown, b in Waldoboro, Me, Oct 22, 1866 He is instructor in Manual Training in Minneapolis, Minn, where they reside

JOHN M Hodgdon[9] (851), b in West Milan, N H, Oct 18, 1848, m. Jan. 2, 1876, Emma Carpenter of Granby, Vt, she d June 13, 1887 He is a carpenter in Davis, W Va He m (2) Nov. 17, 1888, Eva Bell Children

950 Allen W Hodgdon,[10] +
951 Maud Hodgdon,[10] b Sept 16, 1879, d Aug 9, 1882, in West Milan
952 Albert C Hodgdon,[10] +

953 Iola L Hodgdon,[10] +
954 Effie Hodgdon,[10] b May 1, 1891

OZMON M Hodgdon[9] (852), b in West Milan, N H, Mar 1, 1851, m Nov 29, 1879, Cora Carpenter of Granby, Vt He is a farmer in Granby

IOLA A Hodgdon[9] (853), b in West Milan, N H, Dec 10, 1852, m June 16, 1872, John Franklin Thompson of Stark, N H He is a lumberman in Davis, W Va, where they reside. Child

955 Benjamin Frank Thompson,[10] b Sept 28, 1886, d young

DANIEL W Hodgdon[9] (854), b in West Milan, N H, Feb 10, 1855, m Nov, 1875, Rose F Bean of West Milan He is a lumberman in Berlin, N H, where they reside

ERNEST A Hodgdon[9] (855), b in West Milan, N H, Dec 1, 1856, m Oct 18, 1879, Mary A Hogan of Gorham, N H, b in West Frampton, Province of Quebec He is a carpenter in Groveton, N H, where they reside Children

956 Earle W Hodgdon,[10] b in Gorham, N H, June 16, 1884
957 Annie F Hodgdon,[10] b in West Milan, Sept, 1887
958 Grace A Hodgdon,[10] b in West Milan, Jan 15, 1890
958 a Nellie Vail Hodgdon,[10] adopted Sept 30, 1900

MELVIN E Hodgdon[9] (868), b in Milan, N H, Feb 12, 1854, m in Milwaukee, Wis, July 25, 1894, Mrs Emma Eliza (Emerson) Mackie, widow of James Robert Mackie, she was b in Milwaukee, Nov 25, 1862 He is a machinist and resides in Berlin, N H

MARILLA Hodgdon[9] (869), b in West Milan, N H, Aug 17, 1855, m in Gorham, N H, Mar 9, 1882, William Eugene Richards, b in Harmony, Me, Sept 14, 1853 He was a machmist and was killed while working for the Victor Chemical Works in Chicago Heights, Ill, Mar 30, 1903; Mrs Richards resides in Milwaukee, Wis Children

959 Roy William Richards,[10] b in Milwaukee, Aug 22, 1883
960 Ora May Richards,[10] b in Milwaukee, June 27, 1885, d Dec 31, 1890

JOHN A Hodgdon[9] (872), b in West Milan, N H, Apr 24, 1860, m in Portland, Me, Sept 7, 1887, Matilda S, dau of Edward and Hannah (Wheeler) Fernald, b Oct 12, 1867 He is a hardware merchant in Berlin, N H, where they reside Children

961 Gladys Louise Hodgdon,[10] b in Berlin, Sept 25, 1889
962 Emmons Fernald Hodgdon,[10] b in Berlin, July 27, 1891, d Jan 21, 1901
963 Roma Pearl Hodgdon,[10] b in Berlin, Apr 17, 1894
964 Paul Edward Hodgdon,[10] b in Berlin, June 19, 1896
965 A child,[10] b May 26, d June 4, 1900
966 Theodore Alfred Hodgdon,[10] b in Berlin, Mar 10, 1903

HELEN G Hodgdon[9] (873), b in West Milan, N H, Feb 24, 1862, m June 13 1887, Harry Randall Seavey They lived for a time in North Conway, N H, now (1904) in Portland, Me Children

967 Lucia Helen Seavey,[10] b in North Conway, Nov 16 1888
968 Ruby Marion Seavey,[10] b in Portland, Apr 26, 1891
969 Mildred Estelle Seavey,[10] b in Portland, Nov 27, 1899

MINNIE E Hodgdon[9] (874), b in West Milan, N H, Jan 24, 1864, m in Berlin, N H, Nov 23, 1892, Joseph Swift, son of David Oaksman and Elizabeth (Swift) Smiley He is a dry goods merchant in Fitchburg, Mass, where they reside

WALTER F Hodgdon[9] (875), b in West Milan, N H, Jan 19, 1866, m. Jan 19, 1901, Mary Alvena Le Gacy, b in Roxton,

Canada, Oct 15, 1877 They reside in Portland, Me Children.

970 Frances Estelle Hodgdon,[10] b in Biddeford, Me, May 6, 1902

971 Lloyd Earl Hodgdon,[10] b on Long Island, Portland Harbor, Aug 23, 1903

MOSES A Hodgdon[9] (876), b in West Milan, N H, Feb 19, 1868, m at Salamanca, N Y, Oct 20, 1896. Elizabeth Eva, dau of William and Anna (Shack) Decker, b in Wilcox, Pa, Aug 27, 1875 He is a carpenter in Wilcox where they reside Children.

972 Dexter Alberto Hodgdon,[10] b in Wilcox, Oct 13, 1898

973 Minnie Eva Hodgdon,[10] b in Wilcox, Oct 20, 1900

CHARLES D Hodgdon[9] (877), b in West Milan, N H, May 16, 1870, m in Berlin, N H, Aug 19, 1894, Blanch A, dau of Nicholas and Julia (Patterson) Mosher, b in South Alton, Kings Co, Nova Scotia, Nov 7, 1872 He is an engineer in West Milan, where they reside

LEWIS C Hodgdon[9] (878), b in West Milan, N H, Apr 11, 1872, m in Berlin, N H, Dec. 27, 1899, Daphne Editha, dau of Edward and Hannah (Wheeler) Fernald, b in Berlin, Sept 7, 1880 He is a caterer in Berlin, where they reside Child

974 Orville Fernald Hodgdon,[10] b in Berlin, Sept 16, 1901

WILFRED A Hodgdon[9] (880), b in Milan, N H, Jan 30, 1864, m Apr. 5, 1893, Alice Goebel, b Oct 23, 1873 They reside in Berlin, N H Children.

975 Lester Wilfred Hodgdon,[10] b Feb 7, 1894

976 Beatrice Ella Hodgdon,[10] b Mar 17, 1896

977 Viva Elizabeth Hodgdon,[10] b Mar 20, 1897

978 Phyllis Gertrude Hodgdon,[10] b Mar 16, 1899

979 Marie Ethelyn Hodgdon,[10] b Nov 6, 1901

980 Norman John Hodgdon,[10] b Sept 23, 1902

FREDERICK M. HODGDON

EDWARD J. HODGDON

FLORA E. Hodgdon[9] (881), b. in Milan, N. H., Nov. 29, 1865; m. Nov. 28, 1888, Willis Tucker. They reside in Berlin, N. H. Children:

981. Raymond Hodgdon Tucker,[10] b. Jan. 16, 1891.
982. Norma B. Tucker,[10] b. Apr. 28, 1895; d. Aug. 19, 1898.
983. Frank Robley Tucker,[10] b. Aug. 5, 1898.
984. Roma Elizabeth Tucker,[10] b. Aug. 3, 1900.

HENRY Norman Hodgdon[9] (882), b. in Milan, N. H., July 7, 1869; m. Nov. 24, 1897, Emma Littler, b. Aug. 21, 1872. They reside in Berlin, N. H.

JAMES A. G. Adley[9] (884), b. in Dummer, N. H., July 20, 1867; m. Dec. 20, 1888, Angie Jones. They reside in Dummer. Children:

985. James Albert Adley,[10] b. Mar. 20, 1890.
986. Maud Ruth Adley,[10] b. Jan. 7, 1898.
987. Chandler H. Adley,[10] b. Oct. 31, 1901.

FRED M. Hodgdon[9] (886), b. in Farmington, N. H., June 17, 1864; m. in Newmarket, N. H., June 3, 1890, Abigail Shackford, dau. of George Augustus and Abigail (Shackford) Bennett, b. in Newmarket. He is a shoe manufacturer in Haverhill, Mass.

EDWARD J. Hodgdon[9] (887), b. in Brooklyn, N. Y., Oct. 9, 1870; m. in Haverhill, Mass., Sept. 29, 1894, Emily Josephine, dau. of Joshua Weeks and Emily (Wiggin) Nason, b. in Haverhill, May 14, 1877. They reside in Haverhill, where he is a dealer in watches, diamonds and jewelry. Children:

988. Herbert James Hodgdon,[10] b. Nov. 28, 1895.
989. Raymond Fred Hodgdon,[10] b. Oct. 27, 1902.

FRANCES M. Hodgdon[9] (889), b. in Haverhill, Mass., Nov. 9, 1870; m. in Haverhill, Feb. 27, 1891, Fred Fuller, son of Daniel Fuller and Clara Ellen (Fogg) Shedd, b. in New Boston,

N H, Feb 9, 1871 Mr Shedd is editor of the Haverhill Evening Gazette Children:

990 Harold Hodgdon Shedd,[10] b in Haverhill, Jan 6, 1892
991 Clifford Ernest Shedd,[10] b in Haverhill, Nov 21, 1893
992 Karl Eastman Shedd,[10] b in Haverhill, Dec 30, 1894

IDA M Hodgdon[9] (890), b in Livermore, Me, Feb 7, 1864, m in Lyons, Kan, June 25, 1902, John Charles, son of David and Mary Catherine (Dickson) Nicholson, b in Portland Mills, Ind, Jan 2, 1862 They reside in Newton, Kan Child

993 Edith Nicholson,[10] b in Newton, May 15, 1903.

EDITH M Hodgdon[9] (891), b in Haverhill, Mass, Nov 29, 1874, m in Lyons, Kans, June 15, 1904, John Tressler Flickinger They reside in Schenectaday, N Y

GEORGE W Wood[9] (891 b), b in Biddeford, Me, Mar 17, 1854, m. in Fall River, Mass, Chloa Orilla Field, b in Dartmouth, Mass, they lived in Fall River, where she d Feb 24, 1892 Mr Wood now resides in Lawrence, Mass, connected with the cotton mills. Children:

993 a William Horace Wood,[10] +
993 b. Charles Belden Wood,[10] b., d aged two years
993 c George Henry Wood,[10] +
993 d Bertha L Wood,[10] b Feb 20, 1885, d June 18, 1897

LESLIE Low[9] (892), b in New Hampshire, in 1855, when but two years of age his parents settled in Sharon, Wis. He m and lives in Fargo, N Dak.

BELLE Low[9] (893), b in Sharon, Wis, May 29, 1857; being the first white child born in that town, she was given a town lot in honor of the same She m in Brainerd, Minn, Nov 5, 1876, Dr John C Rosser, a brother of General Rosser of the Confederate Army. They reside in West Superior, Wis. Children

HAROLD H. SHEDD

CLIFFORD E. SHEDD KARL E. SHEDD

994 Pearl Rosser,[10] +
995 Ruth Rosser,[10] +
996 Jean Rosser,[10] +
997. Martha Rosser,[10] b Mar 29, 1887
998 John C Rosser, Jr,[10] b Jan 25, 1890

FRED E Low[9] (894), b in Sharon, Wis, Mar 14, 1860, m Fannie Fern Dennin, b in Jamestown, N Y, Aug 15, 1861 Mr Low is city clerk of Brainerd, Minn, also interested in politics Children

999 Belle Low,[10] b in Brainerd, Mar 11, 1880
1000 Marie Low,[10] +
1001 Grace Low,[10] b in Brainerd, Jan 8, 1886
1002 Arthur Eugene Low,[10] b in Brainerd, June 1, 1896

FRANK E Hodgdon[9] (896), b in Sharon, Wis, Jan 7, 1862, m Dec 1, 188–, Maggie Dunn They lived in Duluth, Minn, later in Williston, N Dak Children

1002a Harry Ellsworth Hodgdon,[10] b in Duluth, Oct 31, 1889
1002b George Hodgdon,[10] b in Duluth, Nov 21, 1890
1002c. Frank Hodgdon,[10] b in Duluth, June 18, 1892
1002d Maggie Hodgdon,[10] b in Duluth, Feb 14, 1894
1002e. Jeannette Hodgdon,[10] b in Duluth, Apr 23, 1897, d in Williston, Aug 15, 1897

HARRIET A Hodgdon[9] (898), b in Sharon, Wis, July 7, 1865, m Jan 22, 1887, William R McChesney They lived in St Cloud, Minn, now in Spokane, Wash Child

1092f Belle McChesney,[10] b in St Cloud, Sept 13, 1887

May Hodgdon[9] (899), b in Sharon, Wis, Apr 7, 1867, m Mar 15, 1883, Andrew Bennett Children

1002g Walter Dan Bennett,[10] b May 23, 1884
1002h Finis Maude Bennett,[10] b Feb 2, 1886
1002i Frank Edward Bennett,[10] b Nov 16, 1888

1002j Lucy Leah Bennett,[10] b Dec 18, 1890
1002k Hattie Louise Bennett,[10] b Jan 23, 1892
1002l Andy Henry Bennett,[10] b Dec 17, 1895
1002m Bessie May Bennett,[10] b May 16, 1897, d Apr 6, 1898
1002n Frederick John Bennett,[10] b Mar 23, 1899

MAUDE Hodgdon[9] (900), b in Sharon, Wis, Apr 7, 1867, m Dec 20, 1883, Samuel H Parker They reside in Brainerd, Minn Children

1002o Samuel Howard Parker,[10] b Feb 9, 1886
1002p Ruth Esther Parker,[10] b Feb 4, 1888
1002q Quin Dougall Parker,[10] b Apr 3, 1890
1002r Eunice Jane Parker,[10] b Oct 11, 1893
1002s Marjorie Belle Parker,[10] b Apr 23, 1897

GEORGE A. Hodgdon[9] (903), b in Sharon, Wis, Aug 15, 1875, m Aug 1, 1900, Hattie Hartman They lived in Minot, N Dak, and later in Spokane, Wash Children

1002t Russell Hodgdon,[10] b in Minot, Nov 3, 1901
1002u William Hartman Hodgdon,[10] b in Spokane, May 9, 1903

OLIVE R Hodgdon[9] (904), b in Sharon, Wis, Jan 12, 1878, m Oct 4, 1899, John D McColman

HARRY H Hodgdon[9] (905), b in Janesville, Wis, Nov 10, 1866, m in Ramsey, Ill, Kathern Bolt, they reside in St Louis, Mo

BERTHA F Hodgdon[9] (906), b in Janesville, Wis, Dec 31, 1869, m June 3, 1899, Harry Stacy, they reside in Chicago, Ill

BEULAH A Hodgdon[9] (907), b in Janesville, Wis, Jan 12, 1876, m June 18, 1898, Perry Brown, they reside in Oakland, Cal Child

1003 Marion Brown,[10] b in Oakland, July 26, 1902

EVA Sarasy[9] (908), b in Janesville, Wis, July 10, 1866, m June 14, 1888, K C Lewis, son of Judge Lewis They reside in Juneau, Wis, where he is practicing law

FANNIE Stewart[9] (911), b in Janesville, Wis, Mar 9, 1882, m Dec 29, 1903, Dr R C Morris, they reside in Fort Atkinson, Wis

LESLIE Hagar[9] (914), b in Milan, N H, Apr 22, 1858, m Mar 29, 1896, Octavia M Hodgdon[9] (856), b in Milan, Sept 1, 1877. Child:

1004 Demeritt Watson Hagar,[10] b June 1, 1898

MARY E Nichols[9] (919), b in Milan, N H, Dec 14, 1863, m Jan 17, 1878, Allie Wright, b Jan 17, 1854

CHARLES H Nichols[9] (920), in Milan, N H, Oct 23, 1868, m June 3, 1891, Ella Morrow, b Mar 11, 1869 Children

1005 Augusta Matilda Nichols,[10] b Aug 4, 1893.
1006 Florence Grace Nichols,[10] b July 21, 1900
1007. Elizabeth Muriel Nichols,[10] b June 15, 1902

WILLIAM D Sawyer[9] (921), b in Dover, N H, Nov 26, 1866, m Nov 21, 1890, Susan Gertrude Hall, b in Dover He is a lawyer in New York City, they reside in New Rochelle, N Y Children.

1008 Jonathan Sawyer,[10] b Aug 21, 1891
1009 Elizabeth Bigelow Sawyer,[10] b Jan 24, 1898

CHARLES F Sawyer[9] (922), b in Dover, N H, Jan 16, 1869, m Jan 29, 1895, Gertrude Child Severance, b in San Francisco, Cal He is a woolen manufacturer in Dover, where they reside

JAMES C Sawyer[9] (923), b in Dover, N H, Mar 30, 1872,

m June 10, 1897, Mary Pepperell Frost, b in Dover He is treasurer of Phillips' Academy, Andover, Mass, where they reside Child.

1010 George Frost Sawyer,[10] b June 25, 1902

EDWARD Sawyer[9] (924), b in Dover, N H, July 21, 1874, he is a manufacturer of wire and cable in Stamford, Conn, office in New York City

ALLEN W Hodgdon[10] (950), b in West Milan, N H, June 7, 1877; m Nov 14, 1899, Bertha McGinnis of Granby, Vt, where he is engaged in farming Child.

1011 Florence Hodgdon,[11] b in Granby, Mar 27, 1901

ALBERT C Hodgdon[10] (952), b in West Milan, N H, Sept 7, 1883, m July 19, 1904, Cecille De Pouter He is a farmer in Granby, Vt

IOLA L Hodgdon[10] (953), b in West Milan, N H, Oct 19, 1885, m June 23, 1903, Loren Chappell He is a book-keeper in Victory, Vt, where they reside Child·

1011a. Amanda May Chappell,[11] b May 10, 1904

W HORACE Wood[10] (993a), b. in Fall River, Mass, Feb 9, 1873, m in Lowell, Mass, Sept 8, 1897, Mary, dau of Almond R and Susan J (Shattuck) Lancaster, b in Haverhill, Mass, Dec 27, 1871 He is a musician in Lowell, where they reside

GEORGE H Wood[10] (993c), b in Fall River, Mass, July 17, 1878, m in Methuen, Mass, June 26, 1902, Fannie Isadore, dau of John M and Rebecca (Woodbury) Bailey, b in Haverhill, Mass, Aug 23, 1878 They reside in Methuen, where he is a clerk in a grocery

PEARL Rosser[10] (994), b Oct 7, 1877; m Dec 19, 1896, James Chorls Giggie Child

1012 James Chorls Giggie, Jr,[11] b Jan 6, 1898

RUTH Rosser[10] (995), b Nov 6, 1879, m Sept. 12, 1900, Frank C Brown Children

1013 John Mabbit Brown,[11] b Apr 9, 1902
1014 Thomas L Rosser Brown,[11] b Oct 8, 1903

JEAN Rosser[10] (996), b Aug 30, 1884, m Jan 21, 1903, William R Payton They reside in Duluth, Minn

MARIE Low[10] (1000), b in Brainerd, Minn, Nov 3, 1883, m G W Chadbourne

ISRAEL Hodgdon[5] (359), b in Dover, N H, July 26, 1741, m May 18, 1766, Mary Pearl, b Jan 26, 1747 They settled in Windham, Me Mary d Dec 28, 1827 Israel d Mar 25, 1832 We have but a partial record of his descendants Children.

1015 Moses Hodgdon,[6] +
1016 Aaron Hodgdon,[6] b Oct 28, 1768, d Jan 15, 1770
1017 Sarah Hodgdon,[6] b Dec 16, 1770, m ——— Simons, d July 21, 1843
1018 Abigail Hodgdon,[6] b July 16, 1775, d Jan 17, 1808
1019 Mary Hodgdon,[6] b July 5, 1779, m ——— Gammon
1020 John Hodgdon,[6] } b Aug 13, 1784 d June 11, 1829
1021 Israel Hodgdon,[6] } b Aug 13, 1784 d June 29, 1841
1022 Caleb Hodgdon,[6] } b Jan 21, 1792 d June 10, 1875
1023 Joshua Hodgdon,[6] } b Jan 21, 1792 d July 6, 1808

MOSES Hodsdon[6] (1015), b. in Windham, Me, July 18, 1767, m Phebe, dau of Samuel and Hannah (Jenkins) Hanson, b in 1765, she d in Poland, Me Apr 18, 1814, he d Dec 31, 1853, aged 86 Children

1024 Hanson Hodsdon,[7] b Nov 22, 1786
1025 William Hodsdon,[7] b. Mar 22, 1789
1026 Samuel Hodsdon,[7] b June 10, 1790
1027 Moses Hodsdon,[7] +

1028 Sarah Hodsdon,[7] b Mar 17, 1796
1029 John Hodsdon,[7] b May 17, 1798
1030 Hannah Hodsdon,[7] b Aug 22, 1800.
1031 Mary Hodsdon,[7] b Dec 21, 1802
1032 Phebe Hodsdon,[7] b May 16, 1806

MOSES Hodsdon (1027), b Sept 10, 1794, m Oct 16, 1814, Sally, dau of Mark and Annie (McGuire) Emery, b in Poland, Me, June 26, 1795 They lived in Poland, where she d Dec 25, 1872 Children:

1033 Mark E Hodsdon,[8] +
1034 Martha Ann Hodsdon,[8] +
1035 Burbank Hodsdon,[8] +
1036 Rachel Hodsdon,[8] +
1037 Ellen Hodsdon,[8] +
1038 Lorana Hodsdon,[8] +

MARK E Hodsdon[8] (1033), b in Poland, Me, Feb 27, 1815, m Phebe Getchell, they lived in Poland, where he d about 1869 Child:

1039 Amelia J Hodsdon,[9] +

MARTHA A Hodsdon[8] (1034), b in Poland, Me, m Hira Keene, and they lived in West Poland Children:

1040 Emily Keene,[9] +
1041 Rachel Keene,[9] +
1042 Mark Keene,[9] b 1846, d 1870
1043 Francis Keene,[9] b 1851, d young

BURBANK Hodsdon[8] (1035), b in Poland Me, m and had a family, but we were unable to get the records

RACHEL Hodsdon[8] (1036), b in Poland, Me, m Simon Johnson

ELLEN Hodsdon[8] (1037), b in Poland, Me, m Amaziah

Keene, they live in West Poland, Me Children

1044 Alford B Keene[9] b Aug 31, 1850, d
1045 Andrew A Keene,[9] +
1046 Orren A Keene,[9] +
1047 Rollin A Keene,[9] +
1048 Frank S Keene,[9] +
1049 Emma E Keene,[9] +
1050 Jesse L Keene,[9] +

LORANA Hodsdon[8] (1038), b in Poland, Me, m William E, son of Reuben and Sally (Emery) Blair, b in Poland, Oct 3, 1833 Children

1051 Nellie, Blair,[9] b d
1052 George Blair,[9] +
1053 Addie Blair,[9] +

AMELIA J Hodsdon[9] (1039), b in Poland, Me, Oct 10, 1846, m Dec 22, 1877, Dr Charles Jenkins, b Aug 11, 1844 They live in West Poland, Me

EMILY Keene[9] (1040), b in Poland, Me, Mar 29, 1838, m June 16, 1855, Edwin, son of John and Betsey (Johnson) Emery, b in Poland, Nov 30, 1830 They live in West Poland Children

1054 Anna Emery,[10] +
1055 Carrie Emery,[10] +
1056 William Emery,[10] b July 28, 1878, d Jan 18, 1900

RACHEL Keene[9] (1041), b in Poland, Me, m June 3, 1861, Greenleaf, son of John and Betsey (Johnson) Emery, b in Poland, July 20, 1831 They live in West Paris, Me Children

1057 Bertha Ellen Emery,[10] +
1058 Mertie Inza Emery,[10] +
1059 Warren Ambrose Emery,[10] +
1060 Walter Gerry Emery,[10] +

1061 William Henry Emery,[10] +
1062 Amma K Emery,[10] }
} b Nov 11, 1876
1063 Allie K Emery,[10] }
1064 Leforest Greenleaf Emery,[10] b Mar 17, 1882

ANDREW A Keene[9] (1045), b in Poland, Me, Sept 18, 1852, m Emma Chute Child

1065 George Keene,[10] +

ORREN A Keene[9] (1046), b in Poland, Me, Jan 15, 1854; m Mary Keene Child ·

1066 Nellie Keene,[10]

ROLLIN A Keene[9] (1047), b in Poland, Me, Sept 30, 1858, m Etta Hatch Children:

1067 Ethel Keene,[10] b in 1889.
1068 Forrest Keene,[10] b in 1891
1069 Flora Keene,[10] b in 1893

FRANK S Keene[9] (1048), b in Poland, Me, Oct 4, 1862, m Louisa Tilson Children ·

1070 Almon Keene,[10] b in 1892
1071 Lillian Keene,[10] b in 1893
1072 Fred Keene,[10] b in 1894
1073 Warren Keene,[10] b. in 1896
1074 Grace Keene,[10] b in 1898
1075 Wilber Keene,[10] b in 1903

EMMA E Keene[9] (1049), b in Poland, Me, Feb 28, 1864; m Charles Toby Children

1076 Rudolph Toby,[10] b in 1894
1077 William Toby,[10] b in 1896

JESSE L Keene[9] (1050), b in Poland, Me, Mar 3, 1872, m.

Amy Newport Children

1078 Ruth Keene,[10] b in 1897
1079. Bessie Keene,[10] b in 1899
1080 Doris Keene,[10] b in 1902

GEORGE Blair[9] (1052), b in Poland, Me ; m May Goodwin Children

1081 Georgie Blair,[10] b in 1901
1082 Cecil Blair,[10] b in 1903

ADDIE Blair[9] (1053), b in Poland, Me , m A Boston Children .

1083 Violet Boston,[10] b in 1894
1084 Mary Boston,[10] b in 1900

ANNA Emery[10] (1054), b in Poland, Me , Nov 28, 1856 , m Feb 18, 1878, Alvin D Quimby , they reside in Portland, Me Children .

1085 Addie M Quimby,[11] +
1086. Edwin J Quimby,[11] b Apr 27, 1882
1087 Nellie A Quimby,[11] b July 30, 1889
1088 Percy Quimby,[11] b Oct 18, 1891

CARRIE Emery[10] (1055), b in Poland, Me , Feb 1, 1864 , m Frank Nason , they reside in West Poland

BERTHA E Emery[10] (1057), b in Paris, Me , May 2, 1865 , m in 1888, Julian Stowe , they reside in Paris Child

1089 Derward J Stowe,[11] b in 1896

MERTIE I Emery[10] (1058), b in Paris, Me , Dec 31, 1866 , m in 1881, Leroy Stowe , they reside in Dicksfield, Me Children

1090 Ivan L Stowe,[11] +

1091 Eric C Stowe,[11] b July, 1883.
1092 Oma Stowe,[11] b in 1886
1093 Estella M Stowe,[11] b in 1888
1094. Rachel F. Stowe,[11] b in 1891
1095 Mertie Stowe,[11] b in 1898

WARREN A Emery[10] (1059), b in Paris, Me, Aug 8, 1869, m in 1898, Clyde B Bartlett, they live in Bethel Me

WALTER G Emery[10] (1060), b in Paris, Me, Sept 10, 1871, m in 1901, Ella B Eames they live in Bethel, Me Child

1096 Albert Emery,[11] b. July, 1902.

WILLIAM H Emery[10] (1061), b in Paris, Me, May 26, 1874, m in 1897, May Bryant, they reside in Paris Children

1097 Laura F Emery,[11] b in 1898
1098 Carl G Emery,[11] b in 1900
1099 Trueman S Emery,[11] b Nov 1902
1100 A daughter,[11] b 1904

George Keene[10] (1065), b in Poland, Me, m (name of wife unknown) Children·

1101 A child.[11]
1102 A child [11]

ADDIE M Quimby[11] (1085), b in Portland, Me, Feb 15, 1889, m June 16, 1893, Alfred Grant, they reside in Portland Child·

1103 James Grant,[12] b May 27, 1897

IVAN L Stowe[11] (1090), b in Dicksfield, Me, June, 1882, m Child

1104 A daughter,[12] b in 1904

PETER Hodgdon[5] (360), b in Dover, N H, Oct 18, 1742,

m (1) Dec 11, 1766, Mary, dau of Azariah and Bridget (Bushbie) Boodey, b in Madbury, N H, June 23, 1749, she was twin sister of Capt John Boodey They lived in Nottingham, N H, where Mary d, Oct. 30, 1770, he m (2) July 9, 1772, Patience Chase, b in Kensington, N H, June 26, 1750. We quote the following from the pen of his nephew, Robert Boodey Caverly, the lawyer, poet, and author of the Caverly and Boodey Genealogies —

"Uncle Peter was a nervous, marvellous old gentleman When a lad I saw him once, but can just remember his outlines His dear Molly had gone beyond the river,—we had never seen her He always travelled horse back on his old nag, fleet as the wind Time then had in its toil and trial appeared to hang heavily upon him His aged face had been seamed all over with its cares, his voice appeared cracked and broken, and his wintry locks lay loosely upon his shoulders We can just remember how his veiny hand trembled as he sat at our mother's table feeding himself We remember he spoke of his infirmities as painful to him, saying he used at home a wooden plate, with which to steady his fork But, oh! it would have been music to you to see the old hero come and go"

"Tradition in and about Madbury, among other things, says old Peter's horse, old Bright (by that name he called him), was a wonder among men and colts The common highway was no sort of guide to old Bright, his end and aim was always onward through the shortest way in the shortest time Once given the point of compass, Bright needed no other direction, his course was always in a direct line, straight forward through quagmires, over hedges, fences, brooks, walls and ditches As the venerable charger leaped up and down, old Peter would occasionally be seen in the distance, leaning towards his journey's end, both hands fastened to the mane, his long gray locks tossed by the tempest, and the skirts of his garments at an angle of forty-five degrees, carried back and fluttered by the breeze"

After his first marriage Peter lived in Nottingham, then in Kensington, and in 1778 in Wolfboro, N H, then in Dover until 1790, when he settled in Madbury, where he d Apr 19, 1827

Children :

1105 John Hodgdon,[6] +
1106 Stephen Hodgdon,[6] +
1107 Jonathan Hodgdon,[6] b. in Kensington, Feb 13, 1776, drowned, aged 15
1108 Mary Hodgdon,[6] +
1109 Peter Hodgdon,[6] +
1110 Sarah Hodgdon, +
1111 Chase Hodgdon,[6] +
1112 Lydia Hodgdon,[6] +
1113 Abigail Hodgdon,[6] +
1114 Patience Hodgdon,[6] b in Madbury, June 14, 1793, m Jonathan Jenkins of Madbury, where they lived and died

JOHN Hodgdon[6] (1105), b in Nottingham, N H, Nov 4, 1768, his mother dying when he was less than two years of age, he spent some years of his boyhood with his uncle, Zachariah Boodey, father of Rev Joseph Boodey He m in 1793, Abigail Bickford, b in Barnstead, N H, Apr 9, 1775, he was a farmer in Moultonboro, N H, and the old house still stands upon the hill, outwardly it is unchanged except by the hand of time The farm or a part of it remained in the family, being occupied by his grandson, John Hodsdon, until 1881, making nearly a century. His first wife, Abigail, d Feb 9, 1805. he m (2) Oct 6, 1805, Nancy, dau of Joseph and Phebe (Gowen[5] [552]) Came, b in York, Me, Mar 20, 1777 Mr Hodgdon d May 24, 1818, she lived a widow nearly forty years, dying at the home of her daughter, Irene, Nov 7, 1857, in Moultonboro Children:

1115 Jonathan Hodgdon,[7] +
1116 Mary Hodgdon,[7] b Sept 14, 1796, d. Nov 1807
1117 Charles Hodsdon,[7] +
1118 Elizabeth Hodsdon,[7] +
1119 John Hodsdon,[7] +
1120 Abigail Hodsdon,[7] b Aug 20, 1806, d Sept. 20, 1810

HOMESTEAD OF JOHN HODGDON

1121 Irene Hodsdon,[7] +
1122 Lyman Hodsdon,[7] +
1123 Nathan Green Hodsdon,[7] +
1124 Nancy Gowen Hodsdon,[7] +

STEPHEN Hodgdon[6] (1106), b in Kensington, N H, Mar 16, 1774, m Sally Starbird of Durham, N H, where they lived, and later in Lowell, Mass Children:

1125 Rebecca Hodgdon,[7] b and lived in Lowell
1126 Sarah Hodgdon,[7] b and lived in Lowell
1126a A son,[7] went to New Orleans and never heard from

MARY Hodgdon[6] (1108), b in Wolfboro, N H, Aug 20, 1778, m ——— Chase They lived in Newburyport, where she d Children

1127. Perley Chase[7]
1128 Sarah Chase[7]
1128a Ann Chase,[7] +

PETER Hodgdon[6] (1109), b in Dover, N H, Sept 12, 1781, m Mar. 7, 1816, Judith Drake of Pittsfield, N H, b Mar 12, 1792 They lived in Madbury, N H, and Pittsfield Mr Hodgdon d in 1837, Mrs Hodgdon later lived with her children in Lowell, Mass, and then in Pittsfield, where she d in 1853-4 Children.

1129 James Munro Hodgdon,[7] +
1130 Mary Elizabeth Hodgdon,[7] b in Madbury, Mar 2, 1819, d in 1898
1131 Samuel Gardner Hodgdon,[7] +
1132 Theodate Butters Hodgdon,[7] +
1133. Hannah Ward Hodgdon,[7] +

SARAH Hodgdon[6] (1110), b in Dover, N H, Dec 25, 1783, m Simon, son of Nathan and Mehitable (Stewart) Green of Pittsfield, N H, where they lived and d Children

1134 Nathan Green,[7] b ; d young
1135 Simon Peter Green,[7] b , d young
1136 Sarah Green,[7] b , d young
1137 Charles Oliver Green,[7] m and went West

CHASE Hodgdon[6] (1111), b in Dover, N H , May 19, 1786; m Sally George of Barnstead, N H , they lived and d in Alexandria, N H , where they had a large family of children, a few of whose names we have obtained from other members of the family, but have received no reply from them Children .

1138 Edmund Hodgdon,[7] m and lived in Alexandria
1139 Miles Hodgdon,[7] m and lived in Concord, N H
1140 John Hodgdon,[7] went West and was never heard from
1141 William Hodgdon,[7] lived in Danbury, N H
1142 Martha Hodgdon,[7] m John Atwood of Alexandria
1143 Mary Hodgdon [7]

LYDIA Hodgdon[6] (1112), b in Madbury, N. H., Oct. 7, 1788 , m Joseph Burnham, b Sept 14, 1779 He was a farmer in Durnham, N H , where he d Dec 4, 1867 ; she d Mar 29, 1886 Children .

1144 Lovina Burnham,[7] lived and d in Durham
1145 George Washington Burnham,[7] lived and d in Durham
1146 Sarah A Burnham,[7] lived and d in Durham
1147 John L Burnham,[7] +

ABIGAIL Hodgdon[6] (1113), b in Madbury, N H , Mar 27, 1791 , m Elijah Tuttle of Madbury, where he d. Mrs Tuttle later lived in Wenham, Mass , where she d Mar 7, 1870 Children

1147a Frances Ann Tuttle,[7] +
1147b Peter Hodgdon Tuttle,[7] +
1147c Patience Jane Tuttle,[7] +
1147d George Andrew Tuttle,[7] +

JONATHAN Hodgdon[7] (1115), b in Moultonboro, N H ,

CHARLES HODSDON

Sept 10, 1794; m in Newton, Mass., Oct 3, 1819, Elizabeth Rogers, b in Newton, June 16, 1799 They lived in Newton, where she d June 25, 1855, he d in Western New York Children.

1148 Josiah Rogers Hodgdon,[8] +

1149 Hiram Barney Hodgdon,[8] b in Newton, Oct 16, 1822, d June 22, 1840

1150 Caroline Elizabeth Hodgdon,[8] +

CHARLES Hodsdon,[7] (1117), b in Moultonboro, N H, Nov 28, 1798, m in Moultonboro, in 1820, Hannah, dau of Ammon (?) and Christiana (Paine) Rogers, b in Barnstead, N H, Apr 4, 1796 He was a farmer in Moultonboro, where she d Apr 12, 1864, he d Apr 14, 1878 Children.

1151 John Hodsdon,[8] +

1152 Mary Elizabeth Hodsdon,[8] b June 14, 1825, d Nov, 1839

1153 Abigail Christiana Hodsdon,[8] +

1154 Harriet Rogers Hodsdon,[8] b Feb 6, 1837, d aged 17 months

ELIZABETH Hodsdon[7] (1118), b in Moultonboro, N H, Dec 6, 1800; m (1) Mial Parker of Lowell, Mass, he d and she m (2) Nathaniel Paine of Moultonboro, where she d July 16, 1872 Child

1155 Addison Parker[8], b in Lowell, June 6, 1839, lived in Moultonboro, where he d Mar 3, 1903

JOHN Hodsdon[7] (1119), b in Moultonboro, N H, Mar 9, 1803, m Sept 24, 1831, Lavonia Blanchard They lived in Tewksbury, Mass, where he d Jan 17, 1811, she d Sept 10, 1868 Children.

1156. Abigail B Hodsdon,[8] b May 22, 1832, d Sept 13, 1833

1157 Ann Hodsdon,[8] +

1158 Mary Hodsdon,[8] b Aug 2, 1835, d Mar 17, 1862
1159 John W P Hodsdon,[8] b July 17, 1838, d. Dec. 5, 1843

IRENE Hodsdon[7] (1121), b in Moultonboro, N H, Jan 19, 1808, m in Tuftonboro, N H, Feb 2, 1826, Timothy Fletcher, son of Josiah and Bridget (Fletcher) White, b in Pittsfield, N H, May 7, 1800 They lived in Moultonboro, where he was a butcher and farmer; he d in Moultonboro, Oct 18, 1879 She d in Meredith, N H, Feb 25, 1888 Children:

1160 Annie Fletcher White,[8] +
1161 Mary Preble White,[8] +
1162 Charles Hodsdon White,[8] +
1163 Hannah Came White,[8] +
1164 Lyman Hodsdon White,[8] +
1165 Frances Louisa White,[8] +
1166 Almira Larkin White,[8] +
1167 Elizabeth Nancy White,[8] +
1168 Woodbury Cyrus White,[8] b in Moultonboro, July 4, 1844, enlisted Dec 2, 1861, in Company B, 8th Regiment, New Hampshire Volunteers, d. of fever on Ship Island at the mouth of the Mississippi river in Louisiana, May 12, 1862
1169 Grace Orissa White,[8] +
1170 Mary Whitney White,[8] +

LYMAN Hodsdon[7] (1122), b in Moultonboro, N H, July 21, 1809, m Eliza D, dau of William amd Elizabeth (Came) Brawn, b in Moultonboro, July 23, 1808 He was a farmer in Moultonboro until 1854, when he moved to Merrimack, Sauk Co, Wis, he d in Readsburg, Wis, July 11, 1892, she d in Lakeport, N H Aug, 1894

NATHAN G Hodsdon[7] (1123), b in Moultonboro, N H., Dec 2, 1811, m Abigail W, dau. of Oliver and Hannah (Wadsworth) Hayden, b in Stoughton, Mass, Apr 16, 1815 They

MRS. IRENE (HODSDON) WHITE

TIMOTHY F. WHITE

lived in Stoughton where she d Feb 9, 1876, he d Dec 7, 1896 Children

1171 Elbridge G Hodsdon,[8] b Apr 22, 1835, d young
1172 Susan Aurelia Hodsdon,[8] +
1173 Harriet Augusta Hodsdon,[8] +
1174. Hannah Louisa Hodsdon,[8] +
1175 Abbie Green Hodsdon,[8] +
1176 Franklin Drake Hodsdon,[8] b Sept 19, 1850, d Oct 4, 1851

NANCY G Hodsdon[7] (1124), b in Moultonboro, N H, Sept 23, 1815, m in Boston, Mass, Jan, 1840, Joseph, son of Joseph and Martha (Pierce) Gardner, b in Woburn, Mass, Feb 15, 1810 He was a cabinet maker in Boston where she d Sept 25, 1860, he d in Moultonboro, Oct 14, 1899 Children

1177. Ellen Gardner,[8] b Oct 29, 1841, d Feb 1, 1858
1178 Emma Gardner,[8] b Dec 21, 1846, d in Wisconsin, June 22, 1885
1179. Edith Eliza Gardner,[8] +

JAMES M Hodgdon[7] (1129), b in Madbury, N H, May 20, 1816, m Oct 11, 1842, Hannah Sargent Webster He enlisted a private in Company D, 12th New Hampshire Volunteers, Sept, 1862, he acted as ambulance driver and quartermaster, was honorably discharged at Richmond, Va, July, 1865 They lived in New Hampshire, where Mrs Hodgdon d Jan 4, 1881 In 1888 he went to Seattle, Wash, where he d Jan 31, 1902 Children ·

1180. Josephine E Hodgdon,[8] b in Pittsfield, N H, Feb 13, 1844; now principal of school No 110, New York City
1181 Mary Ann Hodgdon,[8] b in 1848, d Mar 1, 1856
1182 George Naylor Hodgdon,[8] +
1183 James Edward Hodgdon,[8] b in Apr, d Dec 29, 1851
1184 Hannah Ellen Hodgdon,[8] +

SAMUEL G Hodgdon^{7} (1131), b in Madbury, N H, Sept 29, 1820, m in Nashua, N H, Nov 6, 1848, Tabitha Knights Whipple, b in Franconia, N H He was a carpenter in Lowell, Mass, where she d, Jan 20, 1897, he is now living in South Hampton, N H Children

1185 Ella S Hodgdon,^{8} b in 1851, d in 1876

1186. Helen Parker Hodgdon,^{8} b in 1853, d aged 18 months

THEODATE B Hodgdon^{7} (1132), b in Madbury, N H, Sept 15, 1832, m. Johnson Warren, she d in Iowa, in 1899

HANNAH W Hodgdon^{7} (1133), b in Madbury, N H, Apr 23, 1824, m Abraham Spaulding and settled in Montreal, Canada, where she d in 1897 Mr Spaulding is living in Montreal Children

1187 Frederick Abraham Spaulding,^{8} b d young

1188 Annie Ward Spaulding,^{8} + } b in Suncook, N H, Oct 26, 1852

1189 Edward Mortimer Spaulding,^{8} } d

JOHN L Burnham^{7} (1147), b in Durham, N H, Feb 6, 1819, m Dec 22, 1850, Louisa G Whitehouse He was a farmer in Durham, where he d May 18, 1878 Children

1190 Emma L. Burnham,^{8} b Apr. 20, 1852, living in Boston, Mass

1191 Charles L Burnham,^{8} +

FRANCES A Tuttle^{7} (1147a), b in Dover, N H., Jan 29, 1821, m Alfred Showell, b in London, England, Dec 26, 1804 They lived in Lawrence, Mass, where he d Sept 25, 1857, the family resides in Lawrence Children

1191a Alfred Penniman Showell,^{8} b. in Lawrence, Mar 25, 1854, he was clerk in the B and M R R station in Boston, Mass, until 1890, when his health failing he returned to Lawrence

1191b George Addison Showell,[8] b in Lawrence, Oct 18, 1856; he is foreman in the Lawrence Lumber Co

PETER H Tuttle[7] (1147b), b. in Madbury, N H, m in Portsmouth, N H, Ann Elizabeth Ayers, b in Portsmouth In 1855 they moved to Fremont, Wis, where he enlisted in the Union Army, and was killed in the battle of Cold Harbor, Va Mrs Tuttle d in Minneapolis, Minn, Oct., 1894 Children:

1191c Abbie Jane Tuttle,[8] +
1191d Lydia Frances Tuttle,[8] +
1191e Helen Tuttle,[8] +
1191f Mary Tuttle,[8] +
1191g Nettie Tuttle,[8] +
1191h Albert Tuttle,[8] +
1191i George Tuttle,[8] +

PATIENCE J Tuttle[7] (1147c), b in Madbury, N H, m Charles Lyons and lived in Lawrence, Mass, d Apr, 1858 Child.

1191j Nellie Lyons,[8] b in Lawrence, m Charles Cate and d

GEORGE A Tuttle[7] (1147d), b in Madbury, N H, Jan 15, 1832, m June 19, 1862, Mary Helen Richardson, b in Dracut, Mass, Aug 24, 1841 He was a carpenter in Lawrence, Mass, where he d. Dec 24, 1901, the family resides in Lawrence Children

1191k George Moulton Tuttle,[8] b in Lawrence, Mar 15, 1863; he is a carpenter, now salesman in a produce store

1191 l Thaddeus Wendell Tuttle,[8] b in Salem, N H, June 20, 1867, he is a carpenter in Lawrence

JOSIAH R Hodgdon[8] (1148), b in Newton, Mass, Aug 2, 1820, m (1) in Wayland, Mass, Oct 20, 1842, Lucy Frances, b in Wayland, d in Newton, Nov 20, 1847 He m (2) in Ashburnham, Mass, Oct 20, 1849, Sarah H, dau of Elisha, 3rd, and

Juda (Rodgers) White, b in Ashburnham, Nov 12, 1824 They lived in Newton, where she d Dec 20, 1852, he m (3) in Westboro, Mass, Oct 12, 1853, Harriet W Hutchinson, b in Oxford, Mass., Nov 7, 1822 They lived in Newton, where he d Nov 12, 1873 She d in Hyde Park, Mass, Jan 5, 1896 Children.

1192 Frederick Brigham Hodgdon,[9] +

1193 Hiram Dexter Hodgdon,[9] b in Newton, June 23, 1856, d Sept 2, 1857.

1194 Elizabeth Rogers Hodgdon,[9] b in Newton, Mar 6, 1858; d Oct 20, 1872

1195 Caroline Wood Hodgdon,[9] b in Newton, Feb 6, 1860, d. Feb 23, 1875

1196 Harry Sproat Hodgdon,[9] b in Westboro, June 23, d Sept 18, 1868

CAROLINE E Hodgdon[8] (1150), b in Newton, Mass., Dec. 31, 1824, m in Newton, Nov 19, 1846, Solon Alexander, son of Solon and Hannah (Kimball) Clapp, b in Claremont, N H, Apr 27, 1823 They lived for a time in Newton, and later in Hamilton, Ill Child

1197 Solon Francis Clapp,[9] +

JOHN Hodsdon[8] (1151), b in Moultonboro, N H, Dec 18, 1820, m (1) Theodora Belcher of Randolph, Mass He was a farmer in Moultonboro, where she d Aug 2, 1856, aged 29 He m (2) Oct 8, 1857, Mary Jane, dau of David and Sally Fuller (Wallace) Hilton, b in Sandwich, N H, Jan 19, 1839 They lived on the farm in Moultonboro until 1880, when they moved to Meredith, N H, where he d May 6, 1894 The family now (1904) resides in Haverhill, Mass Children

1198 Fred Wilbur Hodsdon,[9] b in Moultonboro, May 13, 1859, d in Waltham, Mass, Nov 26, 1898

1199. John Herman Hodsdon,[9] +

1200 Carrie Lovina Hodsdon,[9] +

1201 Rodney Hilton Hodsdon,[9] +

1202 Jennie Belle Hodsdon,[9] b July 2, 1867, d Sept 8, 1874

1203 Mary Woodman Hodsdon,[9] b Aug 11, 1869, d Apr 17, 1870

1204 Eliza Gertrude Hodsdon,[9] b July 29, 1871, living with her mother in Haverhill

1205 Grace Elizabeth Hodsdon,[9] +

CHRISTINA A Hodsdon[8] (1153), b in Moultonboro, N H, June 10, 1832, m in Sandwich, N H, June 7, 1857, John, son of John and Betsey (Lovejoy) Paine, b in Center Harbor, N H, Oct 26, 1832 He was a farmer in Moultonboro, near Center Harbor village, where he d Mar 4, and his wife Mar 6, 1904, and were buried in one grave Children

1206 Charles Hodsdon Paine,[9] +

1207 Mary Elizabeth Paine,[9] +

1208 Alice Martin Paine,[9] +

1209 Carl Clark Paine,[9] +

1210 Martha Anne Paine,[9] b in Moultonboro, Aug 30, 1876

ANN Hodsdon[8] (1157), b in Lowell, Mass, Oct 19, 1833, m in Lowell, May 7, 1855, Otis Kimball Underwood, b Apr 18, 1833 He was a farmer in Tewksbury, Mass, where she d Sept 23, 1901 Child

1211 Mary E Underwood,[9] +

ANNIE F White[8] (1160), b in Moultonboro, N H, Oct 12, 1826, m in Georgetown, Mass, Nov 7, 1857, True George, son of Jacob and Abigail (Winter) Morrill, b in Salisbury, N H, July 3, 1819 He had had former wife and one son, David M W Morrill, who has a family, is now living in Los Angeles, Cal Mr Morrill was a shoe cutter in Haverhill, Mass, where he d Dec 21, 1865, she d July 25, 1890 Children

1212 Frank True Morrill,[9] +

1213 Leburton Johnson Morrill,[9] b Nov 29, 1860, d Feb 12, 1865

1214 Annie Modesta Morrill,[9] b Feb 24, 1865, d Oct 12, 1882

MARY P White[8] (1161), b in Moultonboro, N. H, Jan 2, 1829; m Jan 6, 1848, Newton, son of Nathan and Nancy (Farwell) Whitney, b in Harvard, Mass, July 26, 1820 He was a descendant of John Whitney,[1] Richard,[2] Moses,[3] Jonas,[4] Jonas,[5] Salmon,[6] Nathan[7] He was an overseer in the cotton mill at Chicopee, Mass, where she d Aug 9, 1849 He m (2) in 1868, Mrs Louisa Hayward They lived on a farm in Holyoke, Mass, where she d Nov 5, 1899, he d Jan 30, 1902 Child.

1215 Myron B Whitney,[9] +

CHARLES H White[8] (1162), b in Moultonboro, N H, Apr 17, 1831, m in Wilton, N H, Nov 27, 1856, Abbie Frances, dau of Charles and Lydia Jones (Burns) Spalding, b in Wilton, Aug 28, 1834 He was a farmer in Wilton, where she d Jan 3, 1904; Mr White now lives in the village at Wilton Children

1216 Emma Lydia White,[9] +
1217 Carroll Spalding White,[9] +
1218 Jennie Frances White,[9] +
1219 Charles Woodbury White,[9] +

HANNAH C White[8] (1163), b in Moultonboro, N H, Apr 13, 1833, m (1) in Lowell, Mass, Feb 11, 1851, Henry J Williams of Lowell, where he was drowned, June 22, 1853 She m. (2) in Boston, Mass, Mar 7, 1863, John E Coates, an upholsterer in Boston, where she resides Children·

1220 Henry Augustus Fletcher Williams,[9] +
1221 May Eloise Coates,[9] +
1222 Maude Elizabeth Coates,[9] b Dec 16, 1884, graduated from the Franklin Grammar school, Boston, 1898, from the High school, June, 1902, and from the Normal school, June, 1904

LYMAN H White[8] (1164), b in Moultonboro, N H, Apr 9, 1835, m (1) July 8, 1855, Sarah Elizabeth, dau of John and —— (Langdon) Dame, b in Guilford, N H, July 11, 1838 He m (2)

CHARLES H. WHITE

MRS. CHARLES H. WHITE

Jan 1, 1864, Sally Bickford of Moultonboro, b Dec 8, 1828 He was a farmer in Moultonboro, where she d Aug 11, 1894 Mr White enlisted, Aug 6, 1861, in company H, 4th regiment New Hampshire Volunteers, under Capt William Badger, for three years Regiment in command of Col Thomas J Whipple, left the state for Washington, D C, Sept 27, 1861, arriving Sept 30, 1861, then to Port Royal, and served in Putnam's brigade, Terry's division, transferred to Bell's brigade, then to Foster's brigade, Ames' division, 10th corps, army of the Carolinas and Potomac Was taken sick and confined in regiment hospital at Hilton Head, South Carolina, about two months, and honorably discharged Jan 24, 1862, on account of surgeon's certificate of disability He is now living in Meredith, N H Children

1223 Andrew Delmar White,[9] +
1224 John Timothy White,[9] +

FRANCES Louisa White[8] (1165), b in Moultonboro, N H, July 6, 1837, m Nov 25, 1870, Josiah, son of Albert and Susan (Russell) Stark, b in Manchester, N H, Dec 21, 1835 He was a machinist in Manchester, where he d Sept 19, 1878, she m (2) Oct 16, 1901, Fred L, son of Theodore and Almira (Sumner) Moody, they reside in Manchester

ALMIRA L White[8] (1166), b in Moultonboro, Dec 9, 1839, author of the "Genealogy of the Descendants of John White of Wenham and Lancaster, Mass," Editor of the "White Family Quarterly" and also of this Genealogy She resides in Haverhill, Mass

ELIZABETH N White[8] (1167), b in Moultonboro, N H, June 12, 1842, m Apr 9, 1890, Charles Coatsworth, son of Art and Lovina B (Clark) Clement, b Dec 15, 1848 He enlisted in Boston, Mass, Apr 19, 1878, in Company K, Capt George M Downey, 21st regiment United States Infantry, Col Henry A Morrow, and served until Apr 18, 1883, when he was discharged at Vancouver Barracks, Washington He re-enlisted in the same company and served five years more and was discharged Apr 18, 1888, at Fort Duchesne, Utah, one hundred miles from Salt Lake City While in service he was in command of Gen. O O Howard, Gen Nelson A Miles and Gen George Crooke, department commanders of the regular army of the United States They live in South Framingham, Mass

GRACE O White[8] (1169), b in Center Harbor, N H, Aug 18, 1847, m in Lowell, Mass, Dec 6, 1871, Charles Henry, son of Samuel H and Eliza D (Whitehouse) Downing, b in Middleton, N H, Oct 26, 1850. They lived in Haverhill, Mass, until 1873, then in Exeter, N H, until 1879, when they returned to Haverhill, remaining until 1901 Now reside in Roxbury, Mass. Children

1225 Ernest Lyman Downing,[9] b in Haverhill, Aug 14, 1872, m Jan 18, 1892, Mary Louise, dau. of Levi and Aurelia (Marcotte) Provencher, b in Haverhill, Dec 23, 1872 They lived for a time in Haverhill, now in Plaistow, N H

1226 Lillian May Downing,[9] b. in Exeter, Mar 26, 1875; d. Apr 29, 1876

1227 Dana Fletcher Downing,[9] b in Exeter, Oct 10, 1877; graduated from the Haverhill High School, 1896 Graduated from Brown University, Providence, R. I, 1900, and from the Boston University Medical School, June 1, 1904 Now practicing in Newton Nervine, West Newton, Mass

1228 Forrest Lincoln Downing,[9] b in Haverhill, Jan 18, 1880, d Nov 6, 1884

1229 Ethel Grace Downing,[9] b in Haverhill, May 12, 1882, living in Roxbury.

MARY W White[8] (1170), b in Moultonboro, N H, Dec 16, 1849, m in Ipswich, Mass, May 16, 1868, Gardner Sleeper, son of Nehemiah and Alice (Maloon) Gilman, b in Charlestown, Vt, Oct 14, 1839 He enlisted in Boston, Mass, Feb, 1865, was in the quartermaster's department, went to Tennessee and Kentucky, was discharged in May, 1865, on account of ill health He is a machinist in Lowell, Mass, where she d Sept 25, 1902 Children

1230 Harold Woodbury Gilman,[9] +
1231 Gracie Irene Gilman,[9] +

SUSAN A Hodsdon[8] (1172), b in Stoughton, Mass, May 20, 1836, m (1) Nov 18, 1852, Nathaniel Merchant of Stoughton He d and she m (2) Dec 2, 1862, Caleb B Marsh, living in Stoughton Child.

1232 Lettie Elouisa Merchant,[9] b Sept 24, 1853; d Sept. 24, 1854

H AUGUSTA Hodsdon[8] (1173), b in Stoughton, Mass, Mar 23, 1838, m. Sept 24, 1855, Benjamin Howard, son of Nathan and Amity (Morton) Atherton, a farmer of Stoughton, where they reside Children.

1233 Harriett Augusta Atherton,[9] +
1234 Benjamin Howard Atherton, Jr,[9] b Apr 2, 1860, d Mar 14, 1881
1235 Nathan Atherton,[9] +
1236 Frank Adams Atherton,[9] +

H LOUISA Hodsdon[8] (1174), b in Stoughton, Mass, Aug 20, 1841, m Nov 3, 1858, Edward A Lunt of Stoughton, where they reside. Children:

1237 Isabelle Louisa Lunt,[9] +
1238 Eddie Freeze Lunt,[9] +

ABBIE G Hodsdon[8] (1175), b in Stoughton, Mass, Jan 25, 1846, m (1) Aug 16, 1862, Alpheus French of Stoughton, m (2) Edmund M Clapp, a lumber man, now retired, they reside in Tiona, Pa Children.

1239 George Allison French,[9] b July 9, 1863.

— 1240 Edmund D Clapp,[9] +
- 1241 Nina Clapp,[9] b July 6, 1887

EDITH E Gardner[8] (1179), b in Boston, Mass, June 15, 1853, m Dec 20, 1876, George Henry, son of Rufus and Nancy (Lovejoy) Smith, b in Moultonboro, N H, June 18, 1847 He was a merchant in Lakeport, N H, where she d Sept 22, 1885, m (2) Jan 23, 1889, Carrie Alice, dau of Wyatt and Hannah (Chick) Bryant, b in Tamworth, N H, Jan 12, 1858, they reside in Lakeport Child

—1242 Harry Lincoln Smith,[9] b in Lake Village (now Lakeport), Feb 12, 1879, living in Lakeport

GEORGE N Hodgdon[8] (1182), b in Pittsfield, N H, July 25, 1850, educated at New Hampton Institution, New Hampton, N H From 1868 to 1872 was in California when he returned to New Hampshire, remaining until 1887, when he settled in Seattle, Wash, and engaged in the lumber business, in 1897, he was elected as a Populist to the Legislature of Washington, where he made a very brilliant record, and won the applause and approval of all good citizens of all parties, for his honest, earnest, energetic and successful work in behalf of the people To him was due the passing of the valued Insurance Policy Law, that has saved the people of Washington thousands of dollars and untold trouble He is a man of ideas, of strong convictions, of untiring energy and absolute honesty, and has received many resolutions and testimonials of appreciations from all over the state He m Sept 14, 1893, Lillian Elizabeth Cudworth, they reside in Seattle Children

1243 Gladys Hodgdon,[9] b July 15, 1894
1244 Lillian Hodgdon,[9] b Apr 13, 1896

HANNAH E Hodgdon[8] (1184), b in Pittsfield, N H, June 8, 1858, m (1) Sept 22, 1875-6, John Emerson Haskins, m (2) June 21, 1900, Albert Alphonso Lovell They reside in Harding,

Mass Children

1245 Arthur Spaulding Haskins,[9] b July 7, 1878
1246 Ethel Grace Haskins,[9] +

ANNIE W. Spaulding[8] (1188), b in Suncook, N H, Oct 26, 1852, m in Montreal, Canada, Mar 13, 1873 Robert Gibson Brown, b in Scotland, Dec, 1839, he d in 1899 She resides in Montreal Children

1246a Roberta Katherine Brown,[9] +
1246b Laurence Spaulding Brown,[9] +
1246c Annie Fredrika Brown,[9] b Sept 29, 1878
1246d Meredith Gibson Brown,[9] b June 22, 1884

CHARLES L Burnham[8] (1191), b in Durham, N H, Sept 30, 1867, m Aug 22, 1887, Annie Shea, they reside in Durham Children

1247 John Burnham,[9] b Nov 17, 1888, d Jan 25, 1889
1247a Harry Burnham,[9] b May 31, 1890

ABBIE J Tuttle[8] (1191c), b in Portsmouth, N H, about 1845, m ——— Wood of Plaistow, N H.

LYDIA F Tuttle[8] (1191d), b in Portsmouth, N H, moved with her parents to Fremont, Wis, in 1854, m in 1870, Joseph C Judkins, and they reside in Yuma, Ariz Children

1247b Willard C. Judkins,[9] b Jan 15, 1872, d in Corona, Cal, May 24, 1898
1247c Charles A Judkins,[9] b Aug 5, 1874, d in Seattle, Wash, Nov 2, 1890
1247d Mabel A Judkins,[9] +
1247e Ralph A Judkins,[9] b Apr 13, 1881
1247f Effie M Judkins,[9] b Nov 19, 1886
1247g George H Judkins,[9] b Apr 30, 1889

HELEN Tuttle[8] (1191e), b in Portsmouth, N H, m in Fremont, Wis, in 1873, D M Evans, they reside in Salem, Ore Children

1247h David Evans,[9] +
1247i Albert Evans,[9] b Dec 3, 1876
1247j Jesse Evans,[9] b June 21, 1881
1247k Victor Evans,[9] b Feb 12, 1885
1247l Ruth Evans,[9] b Mar 29, 1888
1248 Remoth Evans,[9] b Apr 7, 1891

MARY A Tuttle[8] (1191f), b in Wenham, Mass, Sept 26, 1853, moved with her parents to Fremont, Wis, when two years of age, m Nov 10, 1875, Robert W Stoddart They reside in Fond du Lac, Wis Children

1248a Grace M Stoddart,[9] b Aug 27, 1876
1248b Thomas Stoddart,[9] +
1248c Anna Elizabeth Stoddart,[9] b Dec 26, 1881
1248d Jessie Brown Stoddart,[9] b Feb 18, 1886, d Apr 6, 1888
1248e Albert Tuttle Stoddart,[9] b Jan 13, 1888

NETTIE L Tuttle[8] (1191g), b in Fremont, Wis, m in Fond du Lac, Wis, May 21, 1878, Jesse S Hauser They lived in Fond du Lac and Solomon Rapids, Kans, where he d Nov 5, 1885, she m (2) in Salem, Ore, Dec 12, 1888, William H Cook, they reside in Salem Children:

1248f Paul Harold Hauser,[9] b. in Fond du Lac, May 12, 1879, living in Salem, where he has a gun store
1248g Jesse Lloyd Hauser,[9] b. in Solemon Rapids, Jan 16, 1881
1248h Lola Belle Cook,[9] b in Salem, Dec 28, 1890
1248i William Alfred Cook,[9] b June 17, d Dec 11, 1893

ALBERT Tuttle[8] (1191h), b in Fremont, Wis; m and living in Fond du Lac, Wis, where he is in the publishing business Children.

1248j Harold Tuttle [9]
1248k Roy Tuttle [9]
1248l Esther Tuttle [9]

GEORGE Tuttle[8] (1191), b in Fremont, Wis, m ——— He is a minister in the Methodist Episcopal Church, living in Humanville, Mo Children

1248m Ellsworth Tuttle [9]
1248n Marian Tuttle [9]

FREDERICK B Hodgdon[9] (1192), b in Newton, Mass, Aug 2, 1854, m Jan 16, 1878, Flora J Long They have lived in Newton and Worcester and later in Hyde Park, Mass Children:

1249 Caroline Elizabeth Hodgdon,[10] b Dec 7, 1878
1250 Harriet Valentine Hodgdon,[10] b Dec 21, 1880
1251 Harry David Hodgdon,[10] b Mar 27, 1884, d July 27, 1885

SOLON F. Clapp[9] (1197), b in Newton, Mass, Oct 20, 1847, m in Farmington, Iowa, Dec 21, 1883, Clara Meek, b in Farmington, Aug 14, 1849 Child:

1252 Fayette Solon Clapp,[10] b in Keokuk, Iowa, June 21, 1885

J HERMAN Hodsdon[9] (1199), b in Moultonboro, N H, Apr 17, 1861, m in Haverhill, Mass, Nov 7, 1889 Minnie Prescott, dau of David Morrison and Betsey Bean (Prescott) Bachelder, b in Windham, N H, June 2, 1863 Mr Hodsdon is a letter carrier in Haverhill, where they reside Child

1253 Bernard Herman Hodsdon,[10] b Jan 8, 1894

CARRIE L Hodsdon[9] (1200), b in Moultonboro, N H, Feb 9, 1863, m in Boston, Mass, Nov 5, 1895, Valentine Thornton, son of Thomas D and Mary A (Thornton) Sellers, b in Burnley Lancashire, England, in 1856 They reside in Lawrence, Mass.

where he is editor and proprietor of the Lawrence Leader

RODNEY H Hodsdon[9] (1201), b in Moultonboro, N H, Dec 1, 1864, m Apr 29, 1886, Annie M, dau of Newton and Luella D (Atwood) Gray, b in North Woodstock, N H, Aug 23, 1865 They lived in Meredith and Milford, N H, later in Haverhill and Everett, Mass Child.

1254 Howard Rodney Hodsdon,[10] b in Milford, Mar. 2, 1891

GRACE E Hodsdon[9] (1205), b in Moultonboro, N H, Oct 1, 1876, m in Meredith, N H, Oct 7, 1894, John H, son of Timothy S and Margaret (Page) Edgerly, b in Sanbornton, N H, Oct 2, 1867 He is a druggist in Haverhill, Mass, where they reside Child:

1255 Gladys Grace Edgerly,[10] b in Meredith, June 12, 1895.

CHARLES H Paine[9] (1206), b in Moultonboro, N. H., Aug 3, 1858; m in Somerville, Mass, Sept 13, 1880, Mabel M., dau of John and Almasia (Blake) Smith, b in Meredith, N H, Jan 4, 1858 He is a clerk in Government employ, they reside in Somerville Children

1256. Ernest Howard Paine,[10] +
1257 Ethel Maud Paine,[10] b in Laconia, N H, July 22, 1883
1258 John Smith Paine,[10] b in Somerville, Dec 28, 1888

M ELIZABETH Paine[9] (1207), b in Moultonboro, N H., Dec. 30, 1861, m in Dover, N H, May 7, 1890, Ellery Martin, son of Martin V B and Cordelia J (Locke) Felker, b in Barrington, N H, Feb 5, 1868 He is a belt maker in Dover, where they reside

ALICE M Paine[9] (1208), b in Moultonboro, N H, May 4, 1870; m in Ashland, N. H, Mar 28, 1900, Granville, son of Marcus M. and Ann (Pease) Sargent, b in Holderness, N H., Apr 7, 1874 They reside in Center Harbor Village (Moultonboro)

CARL C Paine[9] (1209), b in Moultonboro, N H, Mar 9, 1872, m Jan 1, 1902, Gertrude, dau of Charles M and Ann (Mudgett) Bagley, b in Sandwich, N H, Aug 9, 1878 They reside in Center Harbor, N H

MARY E Underwood[9] (1211), b in Tewksbury, Mass, May 6, 1856, m in Lowell, Mass, Apr 6, 1881, Buzzell King b Apr 8, 1858 They reside in Tewksbury, where he is a cultivator of small fruits Children

1259 Everett H King,[10] b Dec 30, 1882
1260 Blanch King,[10] b Jan 19, 1886
1261 Alice L King,[10] b Apr 25, 1888

FRANK T Morrill[9] (1212), b in Haverhill, Mass, Nov 15, 1858, m in Elgin, Ill, May 24, 1894, Jeanie, dau of John and Christian (Ogilvie) Thomson, b in Aberdeen, Scotland, Sept 9, 1868 They lived for a time in Haverhill, now Wolfboro, N H

MYRON B Whitney[9] (1215), b in Chicopee, Mass, Apr 11, 1849, he was brought up on a farm, educated in the common schools and Commercial college, learned the carpenter's trade, went West about 1885, and settled in St Anthony Park, Minn, as a contractor and builder He m in St Anthony Park, Sept 4, 1887, Henrietta Hale, dau of Dr Henry and Lucy (Hale) Gould, formerly of Norridgewock, Me, b in Woodbury, Minn Oct 6, 1858 They lived for a time in the Park, now in Minneapolis, Minn

EMMA L White[9] (1216), b in Wilton, N H, May 20, 1858, m in Wilton, Oct 13, 1885, Willard N, son of Willard P and Marilla (Gunnison) Griffin, b in Annisquam, Mass, Oct 5, 1862 Mr Griffin is a member of the firm of Griffin Brothers, Wood and Coal Dealers, Gloucester, Mass, where they reside

CARROLL S White[9] (1217), b in Wilton, N H, July 30, 1860, m in Goffstown, N H, Jan 5, 1898, Lizzie Maria, dau of

Francis Fitch and Martha Emily (Merrill) Flint, b in Goffstown, Oct 29, 1873 He was a milk dealer for several years, now a letter carrier in Manchester, N H, where they reside Children:

1262 Orline Emma White,[10] b. in Manchester, Feb 25, 1900
1263 Helen Frances White,[10] b in Manchester, Oct 26, 1902
1264 Dexter Flint White,[10] b in Manchester, Jan 8, 1904

JENNIE F White[9] (1218), b in Wilton, N H, Jan. 25, 1864, m Jan 30, 1889, Las Casas, son of William H and Abby W (Bales) Barnes, b in Wilton, July 20, 1863 He was in a grocery store in Wilton, until the fall of 1895, when he went into business in Milton, Mass, where he d Nov 29, 1895 Mrs Barnes is now living with her father in Wilton Child:

1265 Abbie White Barnes,[10] b in Wilton, Dec 24, 1893

CHARLES W White[9] (1219), b in Wilton, N H., Oct 12, 1868, m in Lyndeboro, N H, June 29, 1893, Lu Abbie, dau of Charles M and Martha M (Weston) Butler, b in Greenfield, N H, Apr 6, 1871 He is a locomotive engineer on the Boston & Maine Railroad They lived for a time in Wilton, now Nashua, N H Children

1266 May Weston White,[10] b in Wilton, Nov 17, 1894
1267 Carroll Butler White,[10] b in Wilton, Dec 4, 1895
1268 Lester Hodsdon White,[10] b in Wilton, Oct 14, 1897
1269 Barbara White,[10] b in Wilton, Oct 25, 1898

HENRY A F Williams[9] (1220), b in Lowell, Mass, Jan 3, 1852, m in Boston, Mass, Oct 8, 1874, Mary Janette, dau of James and Burdette Lawton, b in Binghampton, England, Dec 27, 1851 He was a conductor on the street cars in Boston, d in Moultonboro, N H, July 19, 1876 Mrs Williams resides in Boston Child

1270. Charles Howard Williams,[10] b. June 19, 1875, d Feb. 9, 1876

WHITE FAMILY

ANDREW D. (9) ALFRED H. (11) LYMAN H. (8) ELMER O. (10)

MAY E Coates[9] (1221), b in Boston, Mass, Feb 11, 1867, m in Boston, Oct 16, 1889, Edgar L, son of George J and Mary A (Hall) Rhodes, b in Camden, Me, Dec 11, 1863 He is a member of the firm of Rhodes Bros, Grocery and Provision Dealers, Boston They reside in Dorchester, Mass Children

1271 Helen Eloise Rhodes,[10] b in Boston, Aug 8, 1890
1272 George Henry Rhodes,[10] b in Boston, Feb 21, 1892, d Nov 27, 1894

ANDREW D White[9] (1223), b in Gilford, N H, Apr 4, 1856, m Oct 28, 1872, Myra Melissa, dau of John C and Nancy D (Cotton) Pickering, b in Dover, N H, Dec 5, 1852 He is a farmer in Gilford. Children

1273 Elmer Ora White,[10] +
1274 Oscar White,[10] b in Gilford, Apr 16, 1885

JOHN T White[9] (1224), b in Moultonboro, N H, Sept 28, 1871; m Oct 9, 1893, Nina, dau of Henry and Carrie (Merrill) Piper of Holderness, N H He is a carpenter in Boston, Mass

HAROLD W Gilman[9] (1230), b in Lowell, Mass, July 6, 1869; m July 27, 1896, Fannie Edith, dau of Richard and Delia (Currier) Shannon, b in Lynn, Mass, Sept 3, 1874 They reside in Lowell.

GRACIE I Gilman[9] (1231), b in Lowell, Mass, Aug 27, 1871, m Sept 19, 1892, Walter Brown, son of Dea Albert Brown and Maria (Kilburn) Hall, b in Lowell, Feb 8, 1869 They lived for a time in Lowell, Northbridge and West Warren, Mass, now in Pontiac, R I, where he is superintendent in a cotton mill Child

1275 Richard Gilman Hall,[10] b in Lowell, Dec 16, 1894

HARRIET A. Atherton[9] (1233), b in Stoughton, Mass, Apr 10, 1856, m. in Stoughton, Henry F Smith They reside in

Stoughton Children.

1276 Frederick H Smith,[10] +
1277 Atherton H Smith,[10] b Nov 8, 1888

NATHAN Atherton[9] (1235), b in Stoughton, Mass, Oct 14, 1864, m M Etta Barlow, they live in Stoughton Children

1278 Willis L Atherton,[10] b Aug 7, 1888, d Aug 19, 1889
1279 Nathan C Atherton,[10] b May 31, 1891
1280 Charles C Atherton,[10] b Mar 6, 1893
1281 Robert M Atherton,[10] b June 19, 1896

FRANK A Atherton[9] (1236), b in Stoughton, Mass, June 20, 1868, m June 1, 1899, Mattie D Hunt, they live in Stoughton Child·

1282 Ruth Morrill Atherton,[10] b July 8, 1901

ISABELLE L Lunt[9] (1237), b in Stoughton, Mass, Mar 7, 1860; m Edward Perrin, a dentist in Stoughton, where they reside Children

1283 Hobart Perrin,[10] b Oct 7, 1889
1284 Philipp Perrin,[10] b June 13, 1899

EDDIE F Lunt[9] (1238), b in Stoughton, Mass, Feb 20, 1862, m. Carrie Fage, they live in Stoughton Child

1285 Edward Lunt,[10] b Apr 10, 1893

EDMUND D Clapp[9] (1240), b Sept, 1873, m July 27, 1898, Olive G McKalip, they reside in Oil City, Pa Child

1286 E Donald Clapp,[10] b in Oil City, Dec, 1900

ETHEL G Haskins[9] (1246), b Mar 11, 1881, m Jan 27, 1904, Frank Lee Drummond Rust

ROBERTA K Brown[9] (1246a), b in Montreal, Canada, Jan

1, 1874, m Aug 25, 1898, Charles Hughes, they reside in Montreal Child

1286a Mary Elizabeth Hughes,[10] b Oct 11, 1899

LAURENCE S Brown[9]) 1246b), b in Montreal, Canada, June 12, 1876, m Aug 10, 1899, Maude Hunt, they reside in Montreal Children

1286b Charles Spaulding Brown,[10] b July 16, 1900
1286c Marjorie Annie Brown,[10] b July 31, 1902

MABEL A Judkins[9] (1247d), b Aug 27, 1878, m Aug 14, 1899, Augustus Bush, who was accidentally drowned in Lake Union, Seattle, Wash Mrs Bush d in Yuma, Ariz, Mar 20, 1902

DAVID Evans[9] (1247h), b in Salem, Ore, June 20, 1875, m June, 1904, Alice Yapp, they are living in Fond du Lac, Wis

THOMAS Stoddart[9] (1248b), b in Fond du Lac, Wis, May 16, 1879, m Sept 30, 1903, Minnie E Collins, they reside in Fond du Lac Child

1286d Hazel Marie Stoddart,[10] b June 30, 1904

ERNEST H Paine[10] (1256), b in Boston, Mass, Sept 19, 1881, m in Somerville, Mass, Feb 22, 1904, Annie Jane, dau of William Cornelius and Joanna (McRitchie) Jones, b in Somerville, July 15, 1885 He is employed in a market in Boston, Mass, they reside in Somerville

ELMER O White[10] (1273), b in Gilmantown, N H, May 26, 1879, m Sept 28, 1898, Grace Lydia, dau of Daniel Hoyt and Emily Sophronia (Potter) Rowe, b in Waltham, Mass, Aug 27, 1876 He is a farmer and milk dealer in Guilford Children

1287 Alfred Harold White,[11] b in Gilford, Apr 3, 1900
1288 Clyde Herbert White,[11] b in Gilford, Mar 14, 1902

FREDERICK H Smith[10] (1276), b in Stoughton, Mass, Nov 3, 1875; m Laura Fisher, they reside in Stoughton Child

1289 Harold Smith,[11] b Dec 7, 1896

JOHN Hodgdon[9] (361), b in Dover, N H, Apr 22, 1745, m Jan 22, 1772, Susannah, dau of Joseph and Elizabeth (Tibbetts) Hussey, b in Dover, Jan 28, 1750 From his childhood he was fond of reading, and in one way and another he managed to acquire an excellent practical education, though he attended school but seven days He drew up all his contracts, deeds, bonds, and obligations of every description, was a good land surveyor, made neat plans of his work, and computed the contents by triangulation One of the few amusements of his busy life was the solution of problems in "Thomas' Farmer's Almanac" and in the newspapers of that early day On the 18th of November, 1771, he purchased of Joshua Corliss, for the sum of £217, 16s, the nucleus of the farm at Weare, on which he lived and died A log house then stood on the premises, but he at once erected a small frame house (about 20 x 12 feet, still standing), which soon gave place to the substantial house now (1888) occupied by his grandson, Moses A Hodgdon

John Hodgdon had the usual experience, with rather more than the ordinary success, that attends pioneer life Forests gradually disappeared, barns were built, orchards planted, and by industry and economy, field was added to field, pasture to pasture, until the "Hodgdon farm" became one of the most noted in the country He also owned land in Hillsborough, Antrim, Unity, New Boston, Fishersfield and many other towns In 1799 he purchased of the "Westford & Groton Academy Grant" a large tract of land in the eastern part of Maine, on which the town of Hodgdon now stands In company with others, he purchased unsold lands in an old grant called the "Packer Right," which involved him in much litigation In conducting his numerous lawsuits, he manifested so much skill and ability, that the late Judge Jeremiah Smith once said "I would rather have John Hodgdon associated with me in a land-suit than any lawyer of the New

Hampshire bar." Gov. Samuel Bell, with whom John Hodgdon was associated in real estate transactions, notably one purchase of 31,600 acres in Grafton County, once made a similar statement. Judge Smith and Governor Bell were his council until they were severally raised to the Bench. To a grandson of John Hodgdon, Judge Levi Woodbury once said: "My first case was a land-suit, in which John Hodgdon was plaintiff, and much curiosity was manifested at the bar to see who would be the sucessor of Smith & Bell. The case was well prepared, and the jury gave me a verdict. This case was a great advantage to me, and from that time I had an established reputation, that gave me a very large docket." Many anecdotes are related in which John Hodgdon's ready sarcasm was very effective. On one occasion when he drove up to the court house at Amherst, where a crowd had assembled, a youthful aspirant to legal honors called out in a patronizing tone, "Well, Mr. Hodgdon, so you've come again!" "Yes," he replied, "but if I had no more business here than thee has, I shouldn't come." "We must look out for Mr. Hodgdon's sharp tongue," was a common phrase among the lawyers. Aside from his larger real estate transactions, Mr. Hodgdon bought and stocked many farms for others to cultivate, and was one of the founders of a factory at Hillsborough Bridge, which at one period he carried on alone. He interested himself in improving stock of all kinds. In 1812, he purchased, and brought from Exeter, in his chaise, a Merino buck, about the same time, he bought, on the Connecticut river, a Merino ewe, for which he paid $125, and ten half breed lambs for $300. John Hodgdon was a man of large and powerful frame, about six feet one inch in height, thin but muscular, usually weighing about 212 pounds. In politics he was an openly avowed Federalist, looking more at national than local interests. He had an abiding faith in the simplicity of Christianity as taught by the society of Friends, and was a constant student of its distinctively doctrinal works. He was a man of clear, vigorous intellect, sternly upright, always knew his own mind, and had little patience with indecision and inefficiency. He had an inexhaustible fund of anecdote, was quick in repartee and rhyme, as well as prose, pitiless in his satire against meanness and pretence, but kindly and genial He died Jan 15, 1821, Susannah, his wife, died Dec 6, 1841 Children.

1290 Moses Hodgdon,[6] +
1291 Abigail Hodgdon,[6] +

MOSES Hodgdon[6] (1290), b in Weare, N H, Aug 22, 1773, he received a common school education, was brought up a farmer, and inherited his father's farm He was a man of splendid physique six feet four inches in height, and would weigh two hundred and fifty pounds

He was very energetic and took the lead in all his farming operations. In 1882 Hon John Hodgdon, his son, said of him, "He was the best farmer I ever saw, with him it was always 'Come boys' and everyone readily responded to his call, his energy was contagious" Mr Hodgdon like his father was a member of the Society of Friends, tolerant and liberal minded, generous and sympathetic in deed, but chary in words He was a man of large property, partly inherited from his father, and much increased by himself He was the largest stockholder in Concord bank and had much to do with its affairs He m (1) Nov 8, 1795, Dorcas Neal Dow he m (2) Hannah Roberts Austin, he d Sept 8, 1841 Children

1292 John Hodgdon,[7] +
1293 Abigail Breed Hodgdon,[7] +
1294 Mary Hodgdon,[7] b Aug 27, 1804, d Mar, 1851
1295 Susannah Hodgdon,[7] b Aug 6, 1806. d May 9, 1829
1296 Anna Hodgdon,[7] +
1297 Dorcas Neal Hodgdon,[7] +
1298 Moses Austin Hodgdon,[7] +

ABIGAIL Hodgdon[6] (1291), b in Weare, N H, Aug 7. 1778, m in 1799, Daniel, son of Zephaniah and Ruth (Phillips) Breed, b in Lynn, Mass. Apr 9, 1769 She was his second wife, and d in Weare, Apr 11, 1802

Hon JOHN Hodgdon[7] (1292), b in Weare, N H, Oct 8,

1800, he inherited the sterling integrity of his father, with the executive ability and many personal traits of his grandfather He received his preparatory education at the district school in Weare, Gilmanton Academy and Phillips' Academy in Exeter, N H, entered Bowdoin College in 1823 and graduated with distinguished honors in 1827 He studied law in the office of Allen Gilman of Bangor, Me, and was admitted to the bar in 1830 On the death of his grandfather, in 1821, Mr Hodgdon came into possession of a large tract of land in Maine, and the conditions of ownership demanded immediate attention, he therefore left his studies at Exeter, and, following the water courses and the paths of trappers and Indians, soon reached his grant in northeastern Maine He at once organized a surveying party from the neighboring province of New Brunswick, laid out his land into lots, secured settlers to establish his claim, and thus founded the town which afterwards bore his name In 1832, he was a delegate from Maine to the Democratic National Convention, held in Baltimore, which nominated Andrew Jackson for the presidency In 1833, he was a member of the Governor's council, and, through the influence of the Maine delegation in Washington, he succeeded in establishing a military post at Houlton, Me, and took an active and efficient part in the disputed boundary question which led to the Aroostook war, a controversy finally settled in 1842, by the famous Ashburton treaty Mr Hodgdon held the office of State land agent four years, and that of bank examiner and commissioner six years He was appointed by President Polk commissioner on the part of the State of Maine to confer with a like commission from Massachusetts to settle and distribute the territorial funds In 1846, he was elected to the State senate, and the following year was president of that body He was at one time general of a division of the State militia, hence the title of general, by which he was better known the latter part of his life In 1853, he removed from Maine to Dubuque, Iowa, where he was regarded from the first as a leading and influential man In 1858, he was elected mayor, and in subsequent years filled many positions of trust He was senior warden of the Episcopal church as long as he would consent to an election, and was many times delegate to the national church convention Gen Hodgdon was a thorough partisan, but never narrow or petty, and bestowed his quiet sarcasm on political folly wherever it appeared He was a typical gentleman of the old school, conservative in his tastes, stately in his bearing, somewhat formal in his conversation, but a delightful talker, original and always entertaining In a memorial notice of Gen Hodgdon, he is spoken of as "the noblest Roman of them all," and it is but just to say that his manners, his learning, his character, marked the gentleman, the scholar and the Christian Gen Hodgdon married, in 1838, Margaret Amelia Leggett of New York, they had no children, but adopted a little girl who became the pride and comfort of their lives. He died at Dubuque, Aug 27, 1883

ABIGAIL B Hodgdon[7] (1293), b in Weare, N H, Nov 28, 1802, m Asa Hanson and d in Portland, Me, Aug 9, 1855

ANNA Hodgdon[7] (1296), b in Weare, N H, Apr 20, 1809; m Oct 27, 1831, Nathan, son of John and Eunice (Gove) Sawyer, b in Henniker, N H, Apr 28, 1806 He was in trade with his brother Daniel, at North Weare, a short time, but with this exception has always lived on the old homestead, where he has held many offices of trust She d in 1885 Children

1299 Mary H Sawyer,[8] +
1300 Moses H Sawyer,[8] +

DORCAS N Hodgdon[7] (1297), b in Weare, N H, July 25, 1811, m June 16, 1831, Daniel, son of John and Eunice (Gove) Sawyer, b in Henniker, N H, July 26, 1808 When a young man, he went to Portland, Me, and engaged in wholesale grocery business He remained there until 1838, when he returned to Weare, and for several years sold goods of the Weare Woolen mills In 1848, he opened the first store in North Weare, and continued in business there the rest of his life Mr Sawyer was a typical Quaker, Mrs Sawyer d Apr 26, 1882, he d Apr 8,

1885 Children

1301 Susan H Sawyer,[8] b Nov. 2, 1834, d Jan 24, 1836
1302 Albert H Sawyer,[8] +
1303 Oliver D Sawyer,[8] +
1304 Amelia H. Sawyer,[8] +

MOSES A Hodgdon[7] (1298), b in Weare, N H, June 7, 1817, he received his education at Clinton Grove, Moses A Cartland, teacher, and at the Friend's School, Providence, R I He was one of the most successful farmers in town, for many years extensively engaged in the wood and lumber business in Weare, Derry and Windham, N H, owned many lumber mills, and at one time 6,000 acres of land and also had a half interest in Weare woolen mills He was a member of the republican party from its formation, represented the town in the legislature in 1861-2 and was one of the executive council in 1868-9 A natural leader, he ranked foremost in each of these positions To the integrity of his ancestors, generous impulses and sympathies are added in Mr Hodgdon's nature, and he has ever been a prompt and efficient aid in cases of misfortune For years he was a willing helper in building up the anti-slavery sentiment of his native town, and he has always been a member of the Society of Friends He m (1) June 9, 1842, Abigail Peaslee[7] (1320), who d Nov 30, 1852, he m (2) Mar 31, 1859, Julia Anna, dau of Enoch and Sophronia (Foster) Page of Danvers, Mass Child

1305 Ellen H Hodgdon[8] +

MARY H Sawyer[8] (1299), b in Henniker, N H, May 23, 1833, m Nathan Paige, Jr, of Danvers, Mass They lived in Wakefield, Mass, where he d in 1887

MOSES H Sawyer[8] (1300), b in Henniker, N H, June 8, 1835, m (1) Jan 12, 1867, Emma F Gove of Weare, N H, m (2) Eliza Smith of Henniker He d July 13, 1873

ALBERT H Sawyer[8] (1302), b in Portland, Me, Oct 26,

1837, m Mary Ellen, dau of David and Lydia (Favor) Boynton, b in Weare, N H, Mar 19, 1840 They reside in Weare Child.

1306 Albert O Sawyer,[9] b in 1861

OLIVER D Sawyer[8] (1303), b in Portland, Me, Nov 19, 1839, he was educated at Colby Academy, New London, N H, and at the Friend's School in Providence, R I In 1865, he entered his father's store, remaining with him until his death, and has since successfully carried on the business He was postmaster from 1869 to 1885, and in 1886 elected to the New Hampshire senate for two years. He m Oct. 8, 1884, Mary J Morgan of Hopkinton, N H

AMELIA H Sawyer[8] (1304), b in Weare, N H, Feb 3, 1848, m John William, son of John and Susan D. (Chase) Whittle, b in Weare, May 17, 1843 They reside in North Weare Children

1307 Mary H Whittle,[9] b May 19, 1873.
1308 John A Whittle,[9] b. Feb 18, 1878

ELLEN H Hodgdon[8] (1305), b. in Weare, N H, June 29, 1844, m in 1866, Edward, son of William and Sarah (Buffum) Hill of Yonkers, N Y They reside in Weare Children:

1309 Ellen Elizabeth Hill,[9] b Nov 21, 1869
1310 Edward Buffum Hill,[9] b June 7, 1879
1311 Anne Mary Hill,[9] b Oct 21, 1881
1312 A daughter,[9] b Dec 13, 1885

ABIGAIL Hodgdon[6] (362), b in Dover, N H, Apr 8, 1749, m in 1780, Ebenezer, son of Moses and Mary (Gove) Peaslee Mr Peaslee settled in Weare, N H, in 1772, with neither money nor education to aid him, he was constable and collector for many years, often on important town committees, became a large owner of real estate and the most extensive farmer in town.

He ran a store, hotel, saw and grist-mill, and was a large employer of other men, but never kept any written accounts or made any mistakes in his settlements Always careful of his promises, but prompt to fulfill them, he was just as ready to compel others to fulfill theirs Imagine a tall, broad-shouldered, coarse-featured man, riding on a spirited horse, seldom sitting in his saddle, but standing in the stirrups, invariably riding on the gallop and leaning forward as he rode, wearing a broad-brimmed Quaker hat, turned up in front, hail fellow, well met with everyone, and you have a correct picture of Ebenezer Peaslee He died Dec 17, 1817; she died June 28, 1844 Children

- 1313 Israel Peaslee,[6] +
- 1314 Mary Peaslee,[6] +
- 1315 Moses Peaslee,[6] +
- 1316 Obiadiah Peaslee,[6] b May 19, 1787, d young
- 1317 Betsey Peaslee,[6] +
- 1318 Nancy Peaslee,[6] +
- 1319 Abigail Peaslee,[6] b Apr 6, 1795, d Aug 3, 1873

ISRAEL Peaslee[6] (1313), b in Weare, N H, May 18, 1781, m (1) Anna Austin, who d Nov 9, 1832, m (2) in 1833, Mrs Polly Pattee of Goffstown, N H He was a leading business man in Weare, serving in various town offices He d July 10, 1834 Child

- 1320 Abigail Peaslee,[7] b Aug 23, 1817, m Moses A Hodgdon[7] (1298)

MARY Peaslee[6] (1314), b in Weare, N H, Feb 11, 1783, m James Flanders and settled in Hopkinton, N H He d Nov 11, 1828, she d July 16, 1853 Children

- 1321 Betsey Flanders[7]
- 1322 Ebenezer Flanders,[7] b , m Mercy Holbrook and lived in Henniker, N H
- 1323. Mary Ann Flanders,[7] b , m William Straw and lived in Hopkinton, N H

MOSES Peaslee[6] (1315), b in Weare, N H, Feb 13, 1785, m Mary, dau of Robert and Abigail (Peaslee) Johnson, b in Weare, Feb 13, 1792 He was educated in the old log school-house and later in Kingston Academy and taught school in Weare and the neighboring towns, for several years He was in trade at East Weare then returned to the farm, where he d Nov 14, 1849, she d Sept 13, 1864 Children

1324 Ebenezer Peaslee,[7] +
1325 Robert Peaslee,[7] +
1326 Nancy Peaslee,[7] +

BETSEY Peaslee[6] (1317), b in Weare, N H, Apr 7, 1789, m Daniel Breed of Unity, N H

NANCY Peaslee[6] (1318), b in Weare, N H, Apr 19, 1792, m (1) Dr Samuel, son of Dr Daniel Peterson, b Boscawen, N H, in 1782 He d in Weare, in 1819 She m (2) as his second wife, Charles, son of John and Sarah (Morrill) Chase, they lived in Weare where she d Mar 2, 1862 Children.

1327 Rhoda Chase,[7] +
1328 Israel P Chase,[7] +

EBENEZER Peaslee[7] (1324), b in Weare, N H, July 9, 1816, m in 1842, Rozille A Huntoon of Unity, N H He was an extensive farmer, also engaged in lumber business, taking an active part in town affairs, being several years selectman and moderator. He d in Weare, Nov 2, 1859 Children

1329 Moses R Peaslee,[8] +
1330 Mary Jane Peaslee,[8] +

ROBERT Peaslee[7] (1325), b in Weare, N H, Mar 11, 1818, was educated at Clinton Grove, Hopkinton, N H, and Keene high school, after which he was a teacher for ten winters in Weare, Hopkinton and Sutton, N H He m June 30, 1846, Persis Boardman, dau of Benjamin Dodge of New Boston, N H.

He was a practical surveyor, also a farmer on a part of the old Peaslee homestead, as well as extensively engaged in the manufacturing of lumber Mr. Peaslee was an active participant in town affairs and in preparing the town history He d in Weare, Mar 29, 1898, she d June 5, 1902 Children

1331 Emma Frances Peaslee,[8] +
1332 Ella Maria Peaslee,[8] +
1333 Sarah E Peaslee,[8] b Aug 2, 1852, d Nov 10, 1857
1334 Mary Jane Peaslee,[8] +
1335 Benjamin Dodge Peaslee,[8] +
1336. Charles Henry Peaslee,[8] +
1337 Harland Peaslee,[8] b Dec 23, 1861, d Jan 24, 1862
1338 Fred Peaslee,[8] b Oct 16, 1862, d Jan 29, 1865
1339 Robert James Peaslee,[8] +
1340 Arthur Newton Peaslee,[8] +

NANCY Peaslee[7] (1326), b in Weare, N H, June 8, 1821, m Elijah Frank, son of Charles and Hannah (Huntoon) Gove, b in Weare, May 7, 1819 They lived in Weare, where she d Nov 22, 1853, he m (2) Sarah Connor of Henniker, N H, m (3) Sophia Blanchard of Red Wing, Minn, where they reside Children

1341 Mary Gove,[8] +
1342 Persis Gove,[8] +
1343 Charles Gove,[8] resides in Red Wing

RHODA Chase[7] (1327), b in Weare, N H, in 1824, m Homer F, son of Nathan and Miriam (Frye) Breed, b in Weare, Oct 10, 1823 He is a dealer in wood and lumber at Weare Centre and owns the Chase mills on Centre brook Children

1344 Charles F Breed,[8] b d young
1345 George Breed,[8] b d young

ISRAEL P Chase[7] (1328), b in Weare, N H, Mar 7, 1827, he was for several years editor at Manchester, N H, going from there to California Returning to New Hampshire, he studied medicine with Dr James Peterson of Weare He m Frances S Vose of Francestown, N H , they settled in Virginia, where he was in practice several years, then in Henniker, N H , from which place he removed to Hillsboro Bridge, N H , where he d May 23, 1890; she d July 19, 1890 Children

1346 James P Chase,[8] b Feb 2, 1856, d Nov 1, 1876
1347 Emma Chase,[8] +
1348 Alice Chase,[9] +

MOSES R Peaslee[8] (1329), b in Weare, N H , Mar 14, 1844, m in 1874, Luella H , dau of Ezekiel W and Lovilla (Morse) Moore, b in Weare in 1856 He is a farmer, living on the farm settled by his great grandfather, Ebenezer Peaslee Children

1349 Ebenezer F Peaslee,[9] b Mar 31, 1876
1350 Rosa M Peaslee,[9] b Jan 23, 1879
1351 Moses L Peaslee,[9] b Oct 9, 1881
1352 Frank H Peaslee,[9] b Oct 5, 1883

MARY J Peaslee[8] (1230), b in Weare, N H , June 18, 1845, m Albert O , son of Albert and Phebe (Purington) Vitty, b in Weare, Mar 12, 1846 He is a locomotive engineer, they reside in Windsor, Vt Child.

1353 Guy C Vitty,[9] b Sept 12, 1875

EMMA F Peaslee[8] (1331), b in Weare, N H , Jan 13, 1848, m Sept 14, 1880, Allen Leroy French of Manchester, N H He d Aug 28, 1901, she resides in Manchester

ELLA M Peaslee[8] (1332), b in Weare, N H , Oct 18, 1850, m July 10, 1879, Charles John Hadley They reside in Manchester, N H Children:

1354 John Langdon Hadley,[9] b Apr 3, 1881
1355 Ralph Vincent Hadley,[9] b Mar 16, 1883

MARY J Peaslee[8] (1334), b in Weare, N H, Sept 9, 1854, m Dec 7, 1881, Elton Willis French of Manchester N H They reside in Medford, Mass Children

1356 Edith Mildred French,[9] b Feb 9, 1883
1357 Lucile Grace French,[9] b Nov 6, 1885

BENJAMIN D Peaslee[8] (1335), b in Weare, N H, Apr 18, 1857, he graduated at the Pulte Medical College, Cincinnati, Ohio, in 1885, and began practice in Concord, N H He m (1) Feb 11, 1880, Alice May, dau of Col Samuel B and Eliza A (Clement) Hammond, b in Dunbarton, N H Dec 25, 1858 she d at Hillsboro Bridge, N H, Oct 23, 1887 He m (2) June 11, 1889, Hattie Dutton of Malden, Mass, they reside at Hillsboro Bridge Child

1358 Karl Hammond Peaslee,[9] b Jan 7, 1881, d Sept 26, 1901.

CHARLES H Peaslee[8] (1336), b in Weare, N H, Oct 3, 1859, m (1) Feb 25, 1885, Caddie A Chamberlin of Dunbarton, N H, she d Aug 10, 1887 He m (2) Jan 1, 1889 Susie Rachel Carpenter of Contoocook, N H, where they reside Children

1359 Alice Rachel Peaslee,[9] b Apr 2, 1890
1360 Grace Elizabeth Peaslee,[9] b Aug 30, 1892

ROBERT J Peaslee[8] (1339), b in Weare, N H, Sept 23, 1864, was educated in the common schools of Weare, at Cushing Academy, Ashburnham, Mass, at Arms Academy, Shelburne, Falls, Mass. He studied law with Charles J Hadley of Weare, Burnham & Brown of Manchester, N H, and graduated at the Boston University Law School in 1886 He m Sept 12, 1895, Nellie Dorcas Kimball of Manchester, where he opened a law office in 1887

ARTHUR N Peaslee[8] (1340), b in Weare, N H, Apr 16

1867, he is an Episcopal clergyman, residing in Middletown, R I

MARY Gove[8] (1341), b ———, m George Cotton, they reside at Red Wing, Minn

PERSIS Gove[8] (1342), b ———, m John Jameson, they reside at Red Wing, Minn

EMMA Chase[8] (1347), b July 7, 1859, m in 1891, Charles W Thompson. They reside in Hillsboro Bridge, N H Child:

1361 Elizabeth Thompson,[9] b Nov 4, 1896

ALICE Chase[8] (1348), b Aug 28, 1861, m in 1881, Ira P Smith of Boston, Mass Child

1362 Emma T Smith,[9] b in 1882

INDEX

Lightning Source UK Ltd.
Milton Keynes UK
UKOW021843210213

206644UK00009B/464/P